Everything You Need to Know About the Financial and Legal Aspects of Preparing for Your New Baby

Your
Practical
Pregnancy
Planner

BRETTE McWHORTER SEMBER

McGraw·Hill

New York   Chicago   San Francisco   Lisbon   London   Madrid   Mexico City
Milan   New Delhi   San Juan   Seoul   Singapore   Sydney   Toronto

Library of Congress Cataloging-in-Publication Data

Sember, Brette McWhorter, 1968–
       Your pactical pregnancy planner : everything you need to know about the financial
and legal aspects of preparing for your new baby / Brette McWhorter Sember. —1st ed.
              p.   cm.
       Includes bibliographical references and index.
       ISBN 0-07-143877-7 (book: alk. paper)
              1. Child rearing—Economic aspects—United States.   2. Finance, Personal—
United States.   3. Infants—Care—United States.   4. Parenting—United States.
       I. Title.

       HQ769.S465   2005
       649′.1′0242—dc22   2005010080

ISBN 0-07-143877-7

McGraw-Hill books are available at special quantity discounts to use as premiums and sales
promotions, or for use in corporate training programs. For more information, please write to the
Director of Special Sales, Professional Publishing, McGraw-Hill, Two Penn Plaza, New York, NY
10121-2298. Or contact your local bookstore.

The legal information in this book is designed to give you a broad overview of the current state
of the law about the topics discussed in the book and is provided for basic information. Laws
differ in each state and are constantly evolving and changing, so no book can be completely up
to date and accurate. It is important to consult with an attorney in your state to completely
understand the laws that apply to you and to obtain personal legal advice. This book is not a
substitute for legal advice.

The information in this book that deals with medical, nutritional, and fitness issues is provided
for basic information. You should always consult with your own health care provider about your
own specific case and what is recommended for you. This book is not a substitute for medical
advice.

The information in this book that deals with financial issues is provided for basic information.
You should always consult with your own financial advisor about your own specific situation and
what is recommended for you. This book is not a substitute for financial advice.

The author and publisher disclaim any liability from any claims arising from any information
contained in this book.

This book is printed on acid-free paper.

Contents

Acknowledgments

This book is dedicated to the memory of my grandmother, Olive McWhorter, who believed a woman is never more beautiful than when she is pregnant and who loved children more than anyone else I've ever known. This one's for you, Gram. And the answer is I still don't know.

This book exists due to the genius of my editor, Michele Pezzuti, who asks all the right questions and is available to slap me on the side of the head once in a while when necessary (and whom I still love even though she made me cut pages in the eleventh hour—you get the tough-love award, Michele). The entire team at McGraw-Hill has been terrific, especially those who peppered me with questions to include in the book.

I am grateful to Linda Clark, director of Country Park Child Care, and the Dennis Evchich Insurance Agency for answering my many questions. Thanks also to my own obstetrician, Dr. Maria Corigliano, and pediatrician, Dr. Jean Marfurt, for unwittingly aiding me by answering my numerous ridiculous questions over the years, and to Misty Bott, Sheri Wallace, Megan Buckley, and Dorre Fox.

I remain sane only because my dear friend Belle Wong listened tirelessly to my daily progress through this book. Thanks to my parents, Tom and Kathleen McWhorter, who taught me to ask the probing questions. My love and thanks go to my husband, Terry, and two beautiful children, Quinne and Zayne, who taught me (or learned with me) the lessons in this book.

Introduction

Jennifer recently found out that she is pregnant. She's only eleven weeks along and is not ready to spread the good news around her office yet. Suddenly she is having some problems with her pregnancy. Her doctor assures her that it is likely everything will be just fine, but she needs to go on bed rest for a while. Bed rest? Though the thought of finally getting enough sleep sounds pretty good to her right now, she doesn't know how she's going to manage to keep her job and stay off her feet. She's wondering if she can still get paid, how long her job will be there for her, and whether this will affect how much maternity leave she can take.

Sarah is eight months pregnant with her first child. She has felt kind of superstitious and so hasn't bought anything for the baby yet. Her girlfriends just threw her a shower and now she has more booties and receiving blankets than one baby can ever use, but she still hasn't bought any of the big items the baby is going to need. She went to a baby superstore over the weekend and almost keeled over when she saw how much it all cost. She wishes she had started thinking about how she was going to afford all of this sooner. And on top of that, she's got to come up with a big co-pay when she gives birth. She's wondering how she is going to pay for all of this, what will happen if she can't come up with the money

xiii
...

for the co-pay, and how on earth she's going to be able to buy diapers and baby clothes every month.

When I found out I was pregnant with my first child, I ran straight to the bookstore and felt so happy to be standing in front of all the pregnancy books that I could now finally read. I wanted to know everything about what would be happening to my body, how my baby was growing, and what to do to ensure a safe and healthy delivery. But as a former family attorney, I fortunately had a leg up on some of the other "unexpected" things I would need to know about, and which, to my dismay, I discovered weren't covered in the popular books. There are insurance issues, maternity leave laws, paternity laws, cord blood issues, health insurance privacy laws, genetic testing rights, and much more. I know this sounds a bit overwhelming. We're taught to think that pregnancy is all about pickle and ice cream cravings, bigger bras, and prenatal visits. But there's so much more you'll want—and need—to know, and I'm happy to be able to help you understand some of the rights and legal issues that may become relevant to your pregnancy.

I've written this book to be used as your guide to the questions and concerns that you will deal with throughout your pregnancy for the legal, financial, and practical aspects of planning your baby's life. As a former attorney, I've been asked these questions or have dealt with these topics and felt like it was time that new and expectant parents had a book that addressed all of them. I want this book to answer your questions, provide real solutions, and help you cope with issues that confront new and expectant parents. The book explains the many legal issues that you may face as a new or expectant parent to help you better understand your rights and how best to protect yourself and your family.

When I was pregnant with my two children, I found that dealing with the physical changes of pregnancy was a big concern for me, but I also found that planning for a new baby took a lot more of my time than I expected. Pregnancy wasn't just about growing a big belly but about planning for a major life-changing event. You get to benefit from my experience. I had to hunt down (or learn about the hard way) the resources, tips, and information in this book.

Take this quick quiz to find out how much you really know about your rights.

Answer **T** for true and **F** for false for each statement.

_____ 1. If you have to stop working because of your pregnancy, you will be covered by your state's disability program.

_____ 2. You don't need to worry about taking time off for maternity leave because the Family and Medical Leave Act allows you to take off time without pay and ensures you will have your job waiting for you when you return.

_____ 3. If you want to preserve your baby's cord blood, you should let the hospital know when you go in to deliver.

_____ 4. The hospital can run tests on your newborn baby without your permission or even without telling you about them.

_____ 5. You can set up an IRA (retirement account) for your baby as soon as he or she is born.

_____ 6. After the baby is born, some people will send checks, made out to the baby's name, as gifts. You can't cash these until your child is old enough to sign his or her name or has his or her own bank account.

_____ 7. You can get many baby magazines for free.

_____ 8. It is important to take out a life insurance policy for your baby once he or she is born.

_____ 9. If you and your partner are killed in a car accident on the way home from the hospital, it will be up to a judge to decide who will raise your baby.

_____ 10. You have to give your baby the father's last name.

Answers

1. *False.* Most states do not have disability programs, and you have to hope that your employer has a private disability insurance policy that covers you.

2. *False*. You may not qualify for the FMLA if your employer does not have more than fifty employees or if you have not worked there for more than twelve months. Even if you do qualify you are entitled to only twelve weeks of leave.

3. *False*. You need to make prior arrangements with a cord blood preservation company, sign a contract, and pay them. They will send you the kit and you will need to take it to the hospital with you. If you wait till you're in the hospital to make this decision, it will be too late.

4. *True*. All hospitals have some tests that must be run on newborns that are mandated by state law. These are usually done by pricking the baby's heel and collecting some blood and testing it.

5. *True*. All you need is a social security number and you can start contributing to help your child get a jump on retirement savings.

6. *False*. You can cash these checks yourself and you don't need an account in your child's name.

7. *True*. Several baby magazines are available free to new and expectant parents.

8. *False*. Most financial experts recommend that you invest money rather than pay for a life insurance policy for a child.

9. *True*. If you do not have a will that specifies a guardian, it will be up to a judge to decide who will be your child's guardian.

10. *False*. You can use any last name you like for your baby— yours, your spouse's, a combined name, a hyphenated name, a made-up name, and so on.

Becoming a parent is an exciting journey. You're busy dealing with the changes that pregnancy brings, some of which can feel overwhelming. Nobody expects you to know it all or remember it all. This book is meant to be your resource guide, your reminder, your planner, and your legal guide as you move through pregnancy and into parenthood.

This book is divided into chapters designed to correlate to a specific time in your pregnancy and journey to parenthood. Each chapter deals with topics you may be thinking about, or should be thinking about, during that time period. You should feel free to read ahead or jump around to chapters that interest you. This book will also be an invaluable resource to you after your baby is born. Use the information that you need, when you need it. You may also want to use this book as a reference guide and look things up in the index when you are wondering about them. And, although there was a quiz in this introduction, there's no test at the end of the book!

I'm going to be honest with you and tell you that this book has some information in it that you might not want to think about. No one wants to think about wills, health care directives, miscarriages, pregnancy discrimination, and emergency C-sections. But part of the responsibility of becoming a parent is dealing with important issues that could affect your family. This information is provided so that you can be prepared no matter what and have peace of mind knowing you're armed with the knowledge to confront anything that could happen.

This book is filled with additional resources to help you find more information. *Your Practical Pregnancy Planner* contains the most up-to-date information available, but contact information does change and Web page addresses can change or be redirected. If a Web page listed in this book is no longer available, try doing a search for the information using a search engine such as Google (www.google.com). The websites, organizations, books, and other products or companies listed in this book are not endorsed by the author and are offered for informational purposes only.

The goal of this book is to be inclusive and applicable to married couples, single mothers, gay couples, and unmarried heterosexual couples. So, for the sake of simplicity, the book will often use the word "partner" and may at times use the pronoun "he" when doing so. If these words don't apply to you or your situation, know that the book was written to offer assistance and advice to all types of expectant parents and that information has been included for various situations.

This book often will use the term "your health care provider" instead of "your doctor," since many women use midwives instead of doctors for their prenatal care.

I hope that your pregnancy will be healthy and happy and that your new baby will fill your life with joy.

1

Preconception

*J*udy and her husband have decided they want to have a baby. *Judy believes this is a personal decision and not one that she needs any input on, but her best friend mentioned that she ought to go see her doctor before she starts trying to conceive, since there are some drugs she should stop taking and some supplements she should add to her diet. Another friend then suggested she see a genetic counselor. In addition, when Judy's husband mentioned that he was thinking about moving to a different firm, she began to wonder what would happen if she got pregnant while they were switching to a new insurance company.*

Deciding that you are ready to have a baby is a momentous step—and a very exciting one! You've decided that you want to become a parent and go through the changes that pregnancy brings. The decision to get pregnant is an important milestone, but before you act on it, there are some things you need to do to make sure you are as ready as you can be.

Your Rights

Preconception Medical Care

Doctor visits were once something that came *after* you became pregnant, but now more and more health care providers recommend (but don't require) that you schedule an appointment *before* trying to conceive. The purpose of this appointment is to discuss your general health and any problems you might have conceiving or during pregnancy because of your medical history and also to obtain advice about how to take care of yourself during those few weeks each month when you might be pregnant but can't know for sure yet. At this visit your doctor may prescribe a prenatal vitamin (which he or she will probably recommend you begin taking while you are trying to conceive), talk with you about the importance of getting certain vitamins and minerals in your diet or through supplements, and check your general health to make sure your body is healthy and ready to become pregnant. Your doctor will also talk to you about what medications are safe for you to take while trying to conceive and in early pregnancy. If you are undergoing any treatment such as physical therapy, chiropractic care, herbal medication, or acupuncture, or are taking any prescriptions, be sure to discuss this with your doctor to be sure it is safe to continue. He or she can give you advice about how to conceive quickly and answer any questions or concerns you might have. A preconception visit can also set your mind at ease about your ability to conceive and carry a pregnancy.

Be sure to ask your doctor:

- Which prescription and over-the-counter medications are safe for you to take?
- What diet changes does he or she recommend (such as reducing caffeine and alcohol intake)?
- Are there any activities you should curtail or stop while trying to conceive?
- How could any preexisting medical conditions affect conception or pregnancy?

- How should you calculate your fertile period, and when during your cycle is it best for you to try to conceive?
- How will any hereditary diseases in your family affect you and your pregnancy?

Medications

When you're planning a pregnancy, your doctor may tell you that the best advice is not to take any medication that is not necessary. Always check to make sure an over-the-counter medication is safe before taking it by calling your doctor or talking to your pharmacist. If you are taking any prescription medication, it is essential that you talk with your doctor about whether you should continue. Don't just accept a yes or no answer, though. Ask some of these questions:

- What effect does the drug have on a developing fetus and what are the known possible outcomes if taken during pregnancy? Get statistics so you can evaluate the risk for yourself.
- Is the drug safer during one trimester than another?
- What kind of physical reaction might you have if you stop the medication?
- Are there are alternative medications, herbs, or treatments that are considered safe during pregnancy and could be used in lieu of the medications and treatments you need to stop?

Get two opinions, if possible, for every drug—the doctor who prescribed it and your OB/GYN. Your prescribing doctor may have a better understanding of how the drug works and your OB/GYN may have a better understanding of its effects during conception and pregnancy. It is also important to talk to your doctor about alcohol and caffeine use while you are trying to conceive. He or she will help you understand and evaluate the risks involved.

A list of over-the-counter medications that are considered safe during pregnancy can be found at: www.babycenter.com/general/pregnancytravel/pregnancy/0327.html.

Information about herbal remedies and their safety during pregnancy is available at: www.americanpregnancy.org/pregnancy health/naturalherbsvitamins.html.

Preconception Books and Magazines

Before Your Pregnancy by Amy Ogle (Ballantine Books, 2002, $19.95).

Getting Pregnant: What You Need to Know Right Now by Niels Lauersen (Fireside, 2000, $17.00).

Conceive Magazine (www.conceivemagazine.com, $19.20 per year).

See a Genetic Counselor

Genetic counselors can help you understand the risks of genetic diseases and birth defects, explain how certain medical conditions are inherited, discuss testing options, outline treatments, and calculate probability. The National Society of Genetic Counselors recommends seeing a genetic counselor if:

- You are over 35
- There are serious genetic medical conditions in either of your families
- You had a previous child with abnormalities
- You and/or your partner are known carriers of genetic diseases
- You and your partner are related in some way
- You have had repeated miscarriages

Look for a counselor certified by the American Board of Genetic Counseling. If you are referred to a counselor by your health care provider, the referral should be covered by your health insurance policy. To find a genetic counselor contact the National Society of Genetic Counselors at: www.nsgc.org.

Planning for Self-Employment Disability Leave

If you are self-employed and want postbirth disability coverage or disability leave while pregnant, should you need it, you should consider taking out a disability policy *before* you are pregnant. If you wait until you are pregnant, the pregnancy would be excluded from coverage. Although you can't be denied health insurance because you are pregnant, you can be denied disability insurance.

To qualify, you will be required to provide documentation from your physician and/or undergo a medical exam with an insurance company nurse or doctor to make sure you are in good health. The policy will base disability payments on your average pre-pregnancy income, so you will need to provide documentation of your earnings.

This kind of policy can be a good deal for the self-employed because the policy will pay a percentage of your average monthly income. You pay premiums each month, but once you are collecting benefits, you do not need to pay premiums. You can cancel the policy at any time, so once you've had your baby and collected the benefits, you can cancel it. Taking out this type of policy is a gamble, since you can't be sure you will conceive and actually be able to use the policy for maternity leave. If you become pregnant soon enough, you may end up collecting more in benefits than you paid in premiums. You can cancel the policy as soon as your benefits run out after you have the baby, so that you won't need to pay any more premiums. If it takes a long time to conceive or if your benefits are small, it may not be cost effective to purchase a policy and you might be better off putting money away in a savings or investment account.

Once you get a quote from the insurance company, use the worksheet on the next page to help you calculate whether the policy makes sense for you.

5
· · ·

EVALUATING WHETHER YOU SHOULD BUY A DISABILITY POLICY

Calculate the following to determine if the policy will work well for you:

1. Amount of monthly premium: _____
2. Amount of weekly benefit: _____
3. Monthly premium multiplied by six months (the average length of time it takes to get pregnant): _____
4. Weekly benefit multiplied by six weeks (the average disability period postpartum): _____

If line 3 is more than line 4, you might be better off investing the amount you would have spent on premiums.

If you are concerned about having a longer recovery time or encountering problems during pregnancy that might cause you to be unable to continue working, then the policy may offer you peace of mind in that you will receive payments while being officially "disabled." These policies are also good for any other type of disability; so buying one might be a good idea if you are the primary source of income in your home, if you will be a single parent, or if your family greatly depends on your income. If your insurance agent does not handle this type of coverage (and many do not), contact an insurance broker who can obtain quotes for you from a range of companies.

Paternity Issues
If you are married, your husband is the legal father to a child born to you during the marriage. If you and your husband will be using assisted reproduction to conceive or become parents, there are some things to keep in mind. If you use donated sperm, eggs, or embryos and you carry the baby, the child legally belongs to both

you and your spouse no matter where the genetic material came from, as long as you have used a reproductive rights attorney and have had the appropriate consent forms signed.

If you will be having a baby and you are not married, your partner will need to follow the steps required in your state to admit paternity of the child, which may include registering with a putative father registry or signing a court document admitting paternity. In most states, placing your partner's name on the birth certificate is not enough to completely establish paternity, and a putative father registry is considered to be only one kind of evidence in the steps used to determine paternity.

Find your state law and registry information at: www.crisis pregnancy.com/birth-mother/national-directory-of-putative-father -registries.html or http://naic.acf.hhs.gov/general/legal/statutes/ putativeall.pdf, or contact your state department of social services for family and children for information.

If you have a same-sex partner, she can adopt the child you give birth to. In many states this is a very simple court process. Talk to an adoption attorney about your state's requirements. Read about your state's laws online at: www.lambdalegal.org/cgi-bin/iowa/doc uments/record?record=399.

If you plan to have a baby with a man who does not wish to be involved in the child's life and wishes to have no ties to him or her, you have to understand that even if you agree about this beforehand, there is nothing to stop him from reappearing in your life later and asking for a role in the child's life, unless you see a reproductive rights attorney and have him sign a consent and waiver of all rights before the child is born (and preferably before you conceive!), so that he will be functioning only as a sperm donor. Signing away legal rights does not mean your child can't know who the father is or have some kind of contact with him, but it does solidify your rights as a parent.

If you will be having a child using an anonymous sperm donor, make sure that you use a reputable agency that requires all donors to sign waivers and consents. Some sperm banks will help arrange contact between donors and children once the child becomes an adult.

Choosing Your Baby's Sex

Some people feel very strongly about whether they want a boy or a girl. If you use IVF, your eggs are fertilized in a lab and doctors can select only embryos of one sex to implant. This method has almost 100 percent accuracy (with some room for human error), but is expensive and invasive, since it requires the use of fertility drugs and removal of the eggs from your ovaries.

There is technology available called MicroSort, which will take your partner's sperm and separate out the X and Y sperm. It is (according to their own reports) 90 percent accurate when choosing girls and 74 percent accurate when choosing boys. Once separated, the sperm is then artificially inseminated. The cost is about $3,000 per cycle. This procedure is still being tested by the FDA and has not been approved yet, although it is responsible for over five hundred pregnancies. If you're interested in participating in clinical trials, visit their website at: www.microsort.com.

Your Finances

Planning for Your Medical Costs

Pregnancy is a condition that requires medical care, whether you plan to see an obstetrician or a midwife. Before you become pregnant confirm how much of your pregnancy costs will be covered by health insurance. The average medical cost of a pregnancy is over $4,000 (but worth every penny, of course!). Medical costs include not only prenatal visits but also labor and delivery care, as well as postpartum care. Even if you have a 30 percent co-pay, that's a lot of money.

If you currently have health insurance, pregnancy will be covered, but you should check your policy to find out what co-pays exist and whether you need to use in-network care providers and facilities to get full coverage. If you are a college student, you may be able to obtain insurance through your school. Contact the campus health office for more information.

Your insurance company or your employer cannot cancel your coverage because you are pregnant. If you change health insurance companies (because you change jobs or change policies) during pregnancy, your pregnancy will continue to be covered. The Health Insurance Portability and Accountability Act (HIPAA) states that pregnancy cannot be excluded as a preexisting condition (a medical condition that exists before you enroll in a plan and is not covered by the insurance plan for a period of time). The pregnancy must be covered from the date insurance is effective regardless of when the pregnancy began or what treatment or care has been recommended.

If you leave your job (or if you are covered under your spouse's policy and he leaves his job), you (or he) can choose to continue your health insurance coverage from that employer for up to eighteen months under a law called COBRA (Consolidated Omnibus Budget Reconciliation Act). Under this law you have the right to continue your coverage, but you must pay the premiums your employer was paying. This is an important right because if you leave one job and start another, you will probably have a three-month waiting period before you will become eligible for health insurance through your new employer.

If your employer offers medical insurance and you have not subscribed, ask when the next enrollment period is. Enrollment periods are usually available two or four times per year. It's important to be covered when you do become pregnant so that you can obtain prenatal care right away.

If you have no insurance and none is available to you through employment, check with your state department of health. Many states now offer insurance plans on a sliding scale. You may also be able to join a local chamber of commerce or a professional organization and obtain group coverage rates through them. For example, many local chambers of commerce allow anyone to join their organization, even if they aren't really running a business (normally they just ask you for a business name and contact information). If you are a member of a professional organization or association, your organization may offer health insurance to members at group rates. It is important to find insurance at group rates, because if you approach a health insurance company on your own and try to buy an individual policy, the rates will be much higher.

Dealing with Infertility

Should you find you are having trouble getting pregnant, there are a wide range of treatments available to help you. Talk to your doctor if you have not been able to get pregnant within a year. He or she can discuss testing, options, and treatments with you. What you can afford will affect which path you choose. In most states, insurance companies are not required to provide coverage for fertility treatments. Most companies do provide coverage for diagnosis and treatment of underlying problems that cause infertility (such as fibroids). The following states require some coverage for infertility: Arkansas, California, Connecticut, Hawaii, Illinois, Maryland, Massachusetts, Montana, New York, Ohio, Rhode Island, and Texas.

Check your insurance policy to determine whether it provides coverage for infertility care. Even if coverage is provided, treatments can be denied if they are considered experimental or not medically necessary. You can appeal any denial of coverage. There is the possibility that a denial of coverage for infertility violates the Americans with Disabilities Act (*Kraul v. Iowa Methodist Medical Center* held that infertility meets the definition of disability).

If you do not have coverage, the clinic you work with may offer payment plans or may work with finance companies, allowing you to borrow the money needed to pay for the treatments.

Your Lifestyle

Ovulation Kits

Getting pregnant can be harder than you expect. There are products on the market designed to help you track your ovulation and manage your fertility. Your doctor can recommend an ovulation monitor kit, which is sold over-the-counter in drugstores. You can also use a software program to help track fertility:

- **Ovulation Calendar Pro:** This free software program will generate your personal fertility calendar. Find it at: www .programurl.com/software/pregnancy.htm.
- **Hormonal Forecaster, Femta, and AiS Conception:** These calendar programs are free downloads and help you track your fertility. Find them at: www.handyarchive.com/free/ pregnancy-software.
- **Fertility Friend Online:** This website allows you to chart your fertility, post it on message boards, and keep a journal. Find it at: www.handyarchive.com/free/pregnancy -software.
- **Ovusoft:** This $36.95 program tracks your temperature and cervical mucus and calculates your ovulation date for you. Find it at: www.ovusoft.com.

Pregnancy Tests

If you're going to begin trying to conceive, you'll want to be able to find out when you are pregnant. There are a variety of home pregnancy tests on the market. Generally, the more they cost, the earlier they can detect pregnancy. Check with your doctor to find out what test he or she recommends using. It usually makes sense to buy a two-test kit, since it is rare to get pregnant on your first try. It is important that you have your doctor confirm your pregnancy if a home kit gives you a positive result.

Preconception Checklist
☐ Make a preconception doctor appointment.
☐ Consider purchasing disability insurance if you are self-employed.
☐ Consider the role of your child's father if you are not married.

☐ Check with doctors about all prescription and nonprescription medications you are taking.
☐ Decide if you need to see a genetic counselor.
☐ Check your health insurance status.
☐ Purchase ovulation kits if you feel you need them.
☐ Purchase home pregnancy tests.

2

Month 1

Melody's home pregnancy test was positive. She was very excited but suddenly realized she had many decisions to make. She thought she wanted to work with a midwife instead of a doctor but had no idea how to find one, what to look for, or whether her insurance would cover it since she had just changed jobs. She knew she needed to take a prenatal vitamin but wanted to wait to ask her midwife for a prescription. Her sister had a child with cerebral palsy and she was a bit worried about her own baby's health and whether it was a genetic condition. She was due to get her hair colored but wondered about whether it was safe

Your first month of pregnancy goes by quickly, because by the time you realize or find out you're pregnant, the month is almost gone. When you first find out you are pregnant, a deluge of emotions and thoughts overcome you. Sometimes it can be a bit overwhelming. Suddenly this is no longer something you are wishing for, but something that is happening to you. Be sure to talk about your new feelings with your partner as well as with those close friends and family members you tell about the pregnancy.

to do so while pregnant. She felt it was too early to think about buying anything for the baby, so she just completely put those thoughts out of her mind and did nothing to start planning for those expenses.

Your Rights

Choosing a Health Care Provider

If you have not already chosen a health care provider to see you through your pregnancy, now is the time to do so.

Physician

If you choose a physician, you can choose an obstetrician or a family care specialist. Obstetricians specialize in delivering babies, while family care providers handle all other medical conditions that primary care providers handle. Many women use an OB/GYN, who handles deliveries as well as gynecological checkups and problems. To find a pregnancy caregiver, try these approaches:

- Ask your primary care physician for a recommendation.
- Ask family and friends for recommendations.
- Get the list of participating health care providers from your health insurance company and see who is geographically near you.

Once you have a name, get more information by doing an Internet search using his or her name to find out background information as well as any media coverage relating to him or her. Your state insurance department or medical board may maintain public records of malpractice claims against medical providers. Call and ask how to access this information.

The American Medical Association offers basic information about physicians at: http://dbapps.ama-assn.org/iwcf/iwcfmgr206/ aps?2002024814, including board certifications, medical school, residency, and type of practice. Some states have malpractice records online, so do a search for your state. You can also search state medical board records online at: www.docboard.org.

If you are using an OB, make sure he or she is board certified and is a member of the American College of Obstetricians and Gynecologists. You can use their "Find an Ob-Gyn" service on their website at: www.acog.org.

If you are choosing a new physician, it is a good idea to make an appointment with him or her and try to get a feel as to whether this is a person you will feel comfortable with. Ask these questions:

- How many doctors are in the practice?
- Are there midwives or nurse practitioners who provide prenatal care?
- What is their cutoff gestational age for genetic testing?
- From where did he or she receive his or her degree and what board certifications does he or she have?
- Will you always see your primary doctor or will you rotate through providers on staff?
- Do they take your insurance?
- What days and times are prenatal appointments available?
- What is their C-section rate? Do they do elective C-sections?
- What is their episiotomy rate? What is their forceps/suction delivery rate?
- Do they encourage women to create birth plans? (See Chapter 3.)
- Is someone always on call, and if not, who provides backup?
- At which hospitals does he or she deliver babies? What hospitals will he or she attend in an emergency?
- What is the office's policy on prescription refills? (Some offices will only provide refills by mail or will only accept calls on certain days.)
- Does the doctor have experience dealing with any medical problems or concerns you have?

Midwives

Midwives are professionals who are trained to deliver babies and provide prenatal and postpartum care. There are several types of midwives:

- **Nurse-midwife:** has a nursing degree as well as midwife training
- **Certified nurse-midwife:** has a nursing degree and is certified by the American College of Nurse-Midwives (www.acnm.org)
- **At-large midwife:** does not have a degree but has special training and has been certified by the North American Registry of Midwives (www.narm.org)

When choosing a midwife, ask the following questions:

- What are her training, background, and certification? See above for certification requirements and organizations she should belong to.
- How long has she been a midwife? At least two to three years is recommended.
- How many births does she handle per month? You probably want a midwife who is not overly booked, since you want to be sure she will be available when you go into labor.
- How many births has she handled? Look for a midwife who has attended over fifty births.
- How many clients does she take per month? Look for a midwife who is not completely booked and has room for your birth.
- How can she be reached? Find out if she has a cell phone, answering service, or pager.
- Does she conduct visits at her office or at your home?
- What equipment does she carry with her? Make sure she carries oxygen and resuscitation equipment.

- Is she certified for infant CPR? You want a midwife who is certified.
- Where will she attend births: her office, your home, the hospital, a birth center?
- Who covers for her when she is off duty or at another birth? Backup is essential.
- Does she provide prenatal and postpartum care? This is important for continuity of care.
- What are her fees and what insurance does she accept? Most states require insurance companies to provide coverage for midwife care.
- Is there an obstetrician and hospital she uses for backup? The answer should be yes to both.
- What is her episiotomy rate? An episiotomy rate of over 10 percent is a concern.
- What is her C-section rate? Look for a number under 10 percent.
- What is her forceps or vacuum extraction rate? Look for a rate under 10 percent.
- What is her overall philosophy or outlook about prenatal care and delivery?

Read the Midwives Model of Care, a voluntary professional standard your midwife should follow, online at: www.cfmidwifery .org/mmoc/brochures.aspx.

Doulas

A doula is a trained labor and delivery assistant who provides the mother, her partner, and family with support and encouragement. Doulas are not permitted to perform clinical tasks, such as vaginal exams, fetal monitoring, and so on. A doula does not provide prenatal care, so you will need to select another health care provider to handle that if you plan on having a doula attend your birth. Look for a doula who is a member of Doulas of North America (www.dona.org).

Books About Alternative Health Care Providers

Gentle Birth Choices: A Guide to Making Informed Decisions by Barbara Harper (Healing Art Press, 1994, $16.95).

The Doula Advantage: Your Complete Guide to Having an Empowered and Positive Birth with the Help of a Professional Childbirth Assistant by Rachel Gurevich (Prima, 2003, $12.95).

Other Health Care Providers

During the course of your pregnancy you might find you need to seek out alternative medicine providers such as hypnotists, acupuncturists, and chiropractors. Make sure that any alternative medicine provider you choose has experience working with pregnant women. Be sure to discuss any treatment you receive with your primary pregnancy health care provider.

Your Family Medical History

When you see your health care provider for your first pregnancy visit, he or she will want to take a detailed family medical history. It can be hard to remember exactly what Uncle Sal died of or what kind of cancer your grandmother had as you're sitting in your paper gown on the examining table, so it's a good idea to take some time to think about this in advance or to ask other family members to help you fill in the gaps. Use the worksheet on the next page to fill in any medical conditions you can think of or that you learn about from close relatives and take it with you to your appointment.

It is important to be honest about your own medical history, as well as that of your partner. Be sure to include abortions, stillbirths, miscarriages, pregnancy symptoms, previous pregnancies, sexually transmitted diseases, contraception you were using, drug use (prescription, over-the-counter, and illegal drugs), alcohol use,

FAMILY MEDICAL HISTORY

Your Family's Medical Conditions

Mother: _____

Father: _____

Sister: _____

Sister: _____

Brother: _____

Brother: _____

Maternal grandmother: _____

Maternal grandfather: _____

Maternal aunts and uncles: _____

Maternal cousins: _____

Maternal great-aunts and -uncles: _____

Paternal grandmother: _____

Paternal grandfather: _____

Paternal aunts and uncles: _____

Paternal cousins: _____

Paternal great-aunts and -uncles: _____

Your Spouse's Family's Medical Conditions

Mother: _____

Father: _____

Sister: _____

Sister: _____

Brother: _____

Brother: _____

Maternal grandmother: _____

Maternal grandfather: _____

Maternal aunts and uncles: _____

Maternal cousins: _____

Maternal great-aunts and -uncles: _____

Paternal grandmother: _____

Paternal grandfather: _____

Paternal aunts and uncles: _____

Paternal cousins: _____

Paternal great-aunts and -uncles: _____

smoking, and anything else your health care provider might ask or need to know about.

If you are over thirty-five, or if there are genetic medical conditions in either of your families, and you haven't already done so, you may wish to consider genetic counseling to help understand the risks you face and to help you interpret results from tests done during your pregnancy. Health insurance usually covers genetic counseling if referred by your health care provider. See page 4 for more information about genetic counselors.

Your First Prenatal Appointment

If you haven't already done so, call your health care provider and make your first prenatal appointment. The first visit can be an exciting confirmation of your pregnancy and the first leg of your nine-month journey.

Since this will be your first prenatal appointment, ask some questions when you make the appointment. If you will be seeing an OB/GYN, know that some schedule prenatal appointments in blocks so they see all their pregnant patients at the same time of day. Making your appointment during this block can mean you will be in and out the door more quickly than if you are scheduled between regular GYN patients who are there for yearly visits or are coming in with a problem. These visits can take longer than monthly OB appointments, and if you're scheduled in between them, you may have a longer wait.

Ask if you will be expected to provide a urine sample at every appointment. You may be asked to take a container home with you, which you will be asked to fill and bring to each appointment.

While at the appointment make sure you find out:

- When your due date is (You can also calculate it online at: www.babycenter.com/calculators/duedate.)
- Any special instructions the health care provider recommends for you

- When to return for your next visit
- What vitamins or supplements to take if you aren't already doing so
- What prescription and over-the-counter medications you should discontinue
- If you need any lab work done and if there are any special instructions you need to know about prior (such as fasting)
- If you should get a flu shot while pregnant

Be sure to ask any questions that you have and express any concerns you might be experiencing. Make an appointment for your next visit before you leave.

Your Rights Under Medical Privacy Laws

Now that you're going to be seeing health care providers on a regular basis, it is a good idea to have an understanding about medical privacy laws. On your first visit the office staff will ask you to sign a form acknowledging your understanding of the privacy laws. Most people are too focused on the upcoming appointment to take the time to read and understand what it means.

The Health Insurance Portability and Accountability Act (HIPAA) was designed to help protect patients' privacy rights. The law says that your health care provider or insurance company cannot give out any medical information (verbally or in writing) about you to anyone without your consent.

Information can be shared without your consent to coordinate treatment between health care providers (such as if you are working with a specialist and your primary care doctor) or to obtain payment from insurance. Your information cannot be given to your employer or used in a marketing or advertising campaign without your consent. In order for information to be released to your insurance company, you have to sign a one-time waiver stating that you want your health insurance company to be billed and that you understand that health information will need to be released to them.

21

If you want your spouse or partner to be able to have access to your records (or even to be able to call in with a question on your behalf), tell the office staff you would like to give him written permission to do so. Although the law says that a family member involved in your care can have access to your records, health care providers are very careful about this and want to be certain that you do want your spouse or partner to have access. If you have an unmarried partner, it is essential that you give permission for him to access your records. The office staff will have a form for you to complete. It's a good idea to sign this form at the first visit so that you will have it taken care of.

HIPAA also gives you the right to see your own medical records, obtain a copy of them, and get a report about when and with whom your health information was shared. The law gives you the right to require your health care providers (including hospitals) to make corrections to your medical records or to at least note that you disagree with information included in your record.

If you believe that your medical privacy rights have been violated, contact the U.S. Department of Health and Human Services at: www.hhs.gov/ocr/hipaa, or 866-627-7748.

Your Finances

Health Insurance

Make sure you understand exactly what your health insurance is going to cover during your pregnancy, delivery, and postpartum period. Pull out your benefits manual and check co-pays and deductibles. If you don't have a benefits manual, you can obtain one from your employer's (or your spouse's, if your insurance is through him) human resources department. If the manual does not answer all of your questions, call your health insurance company's customer service number. Ask about coverage and payments for the following:

- Co-pays for office visits and hospital stays
- Specialists, such as genetic counselors or high-risk OBs
- Deductibles (Be sure to find out how it works if your baby will be born in the next calendar year; there are usually yearly deductibles, so you might have to pay a deductible each year during the course of your pregnancy.)
- Prescription coverage (for your prenatal vitamin or any other prescriptions you might need)
- Out-of-network care
- Lab work
- Ultrasounds
- Prenatal classes
- Hospital rooms (fees for semiprivate or private)
- Coverage for nontraditional health care providers, such as midwives and doulas

Make sure you have a list of participating health care providers for your health insurance plan. Depending on your plan, you may have the option of seeing an out-of-network health care provider, but your out-of-pocket costs will be higher. If your health insurance plan only covers network providers, it is probably simplest to use an in-network provider. If you are not willing to change providers and your health care provider is not in your network, ask him or her to join, otherwise all of your health care costs will come directly out of your pocket. You may be able to work out a payment plan with the provider. It may also be worth considering whether or not you qualify for your state health insurance program. Many states have programs that make health insurance available to pregnant women on a sliding fee scale. You will need to be sure your provider is a participating member of the state program.

No matter what plan you're using, confirm that you do not need a referral to see an OB/GYN or a midwife. Most plans allow women to see one of these health care providers in addition to a primary care physician without any referral, but it is important to make sure because if you do not get a referral in advance and your insurance requires it, you may have to pay for the visit yourself. If you do need a referral, obtain one from your primary care physician.

If you have a high deductible, begin to plan for the expense. Call your health care provider and find out how much each prenatal visit costs and make sure you will be able to handle the cost at the time of the visit. If not, ask about available payment plans.

The Health Insurance Portability and Accountability Act (HIPAA) requires that employers who provide health insurance must cover pregnancy and birth-related medical costs in the same way they cover other medical conditions. An additional deductible or separate pay schedule that applies to pregnancy or birth is illegal.

Health Savings Accounts (HSAs)

Health savings accounts are special medical savings accounts that can be created by anyone who has a health insurance plan with a minimum family deductible of $2,000 or a minimum individual deductible of $1,000. You can contribute up to $2,600 for individuals or $5,150 for families per year into the account. The money is placed in the account tax free and must be used to pay medical expenses. Money you do not use each year remains in the account and can be used in later years. Withdrawals not used for health care costs are taxed and subject to a 10 percent penalty.

The key to using an HSA is good record keeping. Whenever you pay for a medical expense, you must keep the receipt so that you have proof the funds were used for medical expenses. Talk with your financial advisor for more information on setting up one of these accounts.

Flexible Spending Accounts (FSAs)

A flexible spending account is set up by your employer. You contribute pretax funds to the account and then you are reimbursed from the account for health care expenses (including any health insurance premiums you pay, health care expenses that are not covered by your insurance plan, and over-the-counter medications, as well as fertility treatments) that you have during the year. Because you do not pay tax on the reimbursement funds, the money is tax free. Depending on your income you may be able to contribute between $2,000 and $5,000 a year to the account. If you do not use the money in the account within the calendar year, you forfeit the balance.

Pregnancy is the perfect time to use an FSA because you know how many visits you will have (ask your provider to specify exactly how often you will be seen) and you can find out the minimum birth costs you will be facing (costs are higher if you have a C-section or complications). Think about when your due date is. If it is in the next calendar year, you might be better served to use an FSA next year and not this year if your expenses will not be high enough. Remember that the FSA money can be used for any health care expenses, not just pregnancy-related expenses, so you might want to use it for new glasses or for a dental cleaning. Funds can also be used for your baby's health care costs.

Use the online FSA calculator to find out if this type of account makes sense for you: www.principal.com/grouplh/selffunded/fsacalculator.htm. Get details about what expenses an FSA can be used for here: www.irs.gov/publications/p502/index.html.

Your Lifestyle

25
• • •

Lifestyle Changes
The American Pregnancy Association recommends avoiding the following during pregnancy:

- **Paint fumes.** Mercury- or lead-based paint can be dangerous to the baby.

- **Changing a cat's litter box.** You could contract toxoplasmosis.
- **Insecticides.** There is the possibility that these could harm the baby.
- **Hot tubs or saunas.** High temperatures are dangerous for the baby.
- **Teeth whitening procedures or do-it-yourself products.** The chemicals in these products can be dangerous to the baby.
- **Botox injections, chemical peels, and collagen injections.** There are no studies, but there is the possibility these could be dangerous for the baby.
- **Some wrinkle creams.** The chemicals in these products could pose a risk. Talk to your health care provider about what you use and find out what her recommendations are.
- **Hair relaxers and hair coloring.** The chemicals used may be dangerous to the baby.
- **Getting or removing amalgam dental fillings.** The mercury in the fillings can be dangerous for the baby. Talk to your dentist about your options.
- **Tanning beds.** High heat can be dangerous for the baby.
- **Self-tanning lotion with DHA in it.** This chemical could be dangerous for the baby.
- **Cigarette smoke.** Smoking, or breathing secondhand smoke, can harm your baby.
- **Amusement park rides.** Many rides will have warning signs, and if you go on these despite them, you assume the risk. These rides can be dangerous because of the violent stops and starts, high pressures, and high forces.
- **Scuba diving.** The decompression process can be dangerous to the baby.

There is also some dispute about the safety of computer emissions during pregnancy. Talk to your health care provider and read about this issue at: www.sheknows.com/about/look/235.htm.

Your health care provider can discuss calories and nutrients with you, or you can ask to see a nutritionist. Your provider may suggest you limit or eliminate the following from your diet (in accordance with the American Pregnancy Association guidelines):

- Fish that is high in mercury (such as tuna and swordfish)
- Undercooked meat
- Unpasteurized honey (which has a risk of botulism)
- Unpasteurized juices
- Deli meat (unless you reheat it before eating)
- Soft cheeses (such as feta, Brie, Camembert, blue-veined cheese, and *queso blanco* because of the risk of Listeria; see: http://vm.cfsan.fda.gov/~dms/listeren.html for more information)
- Nuts, if there is a history of food allergies in your family (if so, this increases your child's risk for food allergies)
- Alcohol
- Undercooked eggs

Creating an Emergency Card

Fill out the emergency card on the next page and keep it in your wallet or purse. You will probably never need it, but being prepared is never a bad idea.

Consider pasting this onto an index card and getting it laminated so that it will last and not get torn. Make sure you write down your health care provider's phone number in an easy-to-find place at home, program it into your cell phone or PDA, and make sure your partner has it programmed into his phone or PDA.

27
···

Buying Pregnancy Books

You've probably got a lot of questions about your changing body, your baby's development, labor, and delivery. Visit your local library and browse the pregnancy books available there or head to the bookstore and buy some. Even though your health care provider is an excellent source of information, it is a good idea to have a few books on hand that can answer questions you have and tell you what to expect throughout your pregnancy.

Emergency Contact Information

My name is _____. My date of birth is _____.

I am pregnant with a due date of _____.

I take the following medications: _____.

My blood type is _____.

I am allergic to _____.

My primary care provider is _____.
name and phone

My OB/midwife is _____.
name and phone

In case of emergency please contact _____
name and phone

_____ or _____.
name and phone

Pregnancy Books

Books for Moms
What to Expect When You're Expecting by Heidi Murkoff (Workman, 2002, $13.95).

The Girlfriends' Guide to Pregnancy by Vicki Iovine (Pocket Books, 1995, $14.00).

The Mother of All Pregnancy Books by Ann Douglas (John Wiley and Sons, 2002, $15.99).

The Pregnancy Book by Martha Sears (Little, Brown and Company, 1997, $13.95).

The *Pregnancy Bible* by Joanne Stone (Firefly, 2003, $29.95).

Your Pregnancy Week by Week by Glade B. Curtis (De Capo, 2004, $15.95).

Books for Dads
The Expectant Father: Facts, Tips and Advice for Dads-To-Be by Armin A. Brott (Abbeville, 2001, $11.95).

My Boys Can Swim!: The Official Guy's Guide to Pregnancy by Ian Davis (Prima Lifestyles, 1999, $9.99).

Starting a Pregnancy Journal

Many women like to keep a pregnancy journal that allows them to remember this wonderful time and also provides a way to preserve their thoughts so that they can one day share them with their child. You can start your own journal in a notebook, cloth-covered blank book, or computer file, or you can buy a pregnancy journal.

Pregnancy Journals
Butterflies and Hiccups: A Guided Pregnancy Journal by Laurie Wing (New Beginnings Production Company, 2002, $19.95).

An Expectant Mother's Journal by Angela Thomas Guffey (Honor Books, 2001, $12.95).

Your Pregnancy Journal Week by Week by Glade B. Curtis (Perseus Publishing, 2002, $15.95).

Expecting You: My Pregnancy Journal by Linda Kranz (Perseus Publishing, 2000, $15.95).

My Pregnancy: A Record Book (Havoc Publishing, 1998, $20.00).

You might want to include the following in your journal:

- Changes in your body
- Cravings
- Hopes and wishes for the baby
- Your emotions throughout the pregnancy
- Milestones, such as how you found out you were pregnant or the baby's first kick
- How you told others about your pregnancy

Month 1 Checklist

- ☐ Choose a health care provider for your pregnancy.
- ☐ Prepare a family medical history.
- ☐ Schedule a prenatal appointment.
- ☐ Calculate or learn your due date.
- ☐ Sign waivers for the insurance company to allow your partner access to your records.
- ☐ Obtain details about co-pays, coverage, and deductibles from your health insurance company.
- ☐ Open a health savings account if you qualify.
- ☐ Open a flexible spending account if offered by your employer.
- ☐ Make lifestyle changes.
- ☐ Fill out an emergency card and put it in your wallet or purse.
- ☐ Place your health care provider's phone number in an easy-to-find location at home and program it into cell phones and PDAs.
- ☐ Buy and begin reading pregnancy books.
- ☐ Start a pregnancy journal.

3

Month 2

Miranda was in her second month of pregnancy and was so sick she couldn't even think about food, well, unless she was thinking about rye bread with mayo on it, since that was the only thing that appealed to her. She mostly felt sick in the mornings. By afternoon her nausea at least wasn't doubling her over. She worked as an in-house sales representative. At first she tried to go to work every morning at 9:00 but soon she just couldn't drag herself out of bed. She started to come in late and eventually her supervisor confronted her about her tardiness. Suddenly she was on probation. Fortunately she started to feel better soon, but because of her past tardiness she was still on probation. She

As month two moves along you will probably start to feel more used to the idea of being pregnant. You may hear your baby's heart beating by now, something that always brings home the reality of the situation. This month is a good time to start thinking about a birth plan, join an online due date club, and subscribe to pregnancy magazines.

realized maybe she hadn't handled things the right way and should have taken the bull by the horns and talked to her supervisor about her problem before it screwed up her chances for a promotion.

Your Rights

Birth Plan

One of the most important things you can do this month is begin to think about what type of birth experience you want to have. This isn't a decision you will want to make lightly, and you may find that it is a decision that will slowly come together for you as you think it over and discuss it. Talk to your health care provider and your partner and do some reading to learn about the different options. Don't feel pressured to make this decision immediately. Instead give yourself some time to work through the choices in your mind.

A birth plan is a written outline of how you would like to experience the birth process. It includes information about your preferences including:

- **Home birth.** Some women definitely want a home birth, others are definitely against it, while many more women really are unsure.
- **Birth centers.** Find out if there are any in your area and if they are run by midwives or are connected to a hospital. A birth center can provide a comfortable environment for birth.
- **Water birth.** These are available at birth centers, or you can buy a special tub for home birth.
- **Birth positions and birth furniture.** Furniture includes birthing stools, balls, and chairs. Birth positions will be discussed in your pregnancy books and in your prenatal class.

- **Anesthesia options.** There are a wide variety of options available today, and you will want to educate yourself about epidurals and pain relievers.
- **Episiotomies.** Talk to your health care provider about this decision.
- **Comfort measures during labor, such as music, massage, and lighting.** Find out what options are available and consider what you think would work best for you.
- **Length of stay in the hospital.** Some women want to leave as soon as possible, while others want to stay and have help caring for the baby.
- **Use of birth assistants.** You may wish to use a doula or midwife to help with your labor.
- **Who is present in the room with you.** Do you want just your labor coach, or would you like your family and friends too?
- **Whether you consent to residents or interns observing.** Ask your provider what the policy is.
- **Use of film or photography during the birth.** Consider how you would feel most comfortable.
- **Fetal monitoring methods.** Internal and external monitors are available.
- **IV and fluid intake.** Will you consent to an IV? Do you want to be able to eat ice chips?
- **Glasses or contacts.** You may have to take your contacts out in case you need a C-section. Find out the policy in advance and decide what you will do if you have corrected vision.
- **Mobility.** Think about how mobile you want to be during labor, with freedom to walk the halls. Fetal monitoring and IVs limit mobility.
- **Rupture of membranes.** This can help speed labor up but creates a specific window during which you must give birth or face a C-section to prevent possible infection.
- **Labor augmentation (pitocin or prostaglandin).** These drugs can help speed up labor but can make labor more

intense. Think about whether you are opposed to their use or not.

- **Mirror to view the birth.** Some facilities can place a mirror so that you can see the birth.
- **Contact with baby after birth.** Do you want to have bonding time with the baby immediately after the birth, or is it OK with you if the baby goes straight to the nursery?
- **Rooming-in.** This means the baby will stay in your room instead of in the nursery. Some mothers want to sleep and rest while others want to be with their baby all the time.
- **Breast- or bottle-feeding.** When you enter the hospital, specify your preferences and make sure your baby isn't given formula if you want to breastfeed.
- **Pacifier use.** It is standard in most hospitals for babies to be given pacifiers, but if you don't want your baby to have one, you can specify this. Some parents prefer not to use them, since pacifiers can create problems with developing teeth and can be difficult to get rid of when the baby is older, although some studies have shown they help reduce SIDS (Sudden Infant Death Syndrome).
- **Circumcision.** The choice about circumcision is a personal one. See Chapter 9 for more information.
- **Cutting the cord.** Some women want to do this themselves, some want their labor coach to do it, and some prefer that their health care provider handle it.
- **Planned C-section.** If you want a planned C-section, this is something to discuss with your obstetrician.
- **Emergency C-section.** In case of an emergency C-section, make clear your preferences about anesthesia, incisions, and having your partner with you.

When you create a birth plan you should consider all the alternatives and options available to you and discuss them with your health care provider and partner. At this point in your pregnancy you probably don't know the answers to all of the issues a birth plan normally covers, but it is time to begin educating yourself about the options and considering your reactions to all of them. Take some time to consider the choices.

You can create a birth plan online at: http://birthplan.com or www.childbirth.org/interactive/ibirthplan.html.

Find more information about birth plan choices at:

- www.dona.org (Doulas of North America)
- www.waterbirth.org (information about water birth)
- www.caringforkids.cps.ca/babies/Pacifiers.htm (information about pacifiers)
- www.lalecheleague.org (information about breastfeeding)
- www.gentlebirth.org/archives/comfort.html (comfort measures during labor)
- www.childbirth.org/articles/epis.html (information about episiotomies)
- www.lamaze.com (information about birth position, comfort measures, and breathing)

Whatever birth plan you decide on, you must understand that it is not going to be written in stone. Obviously, there are many aspects of your baby's birth that you won't be able to plan or control. A birth plan offers your health care provider an indication of your preferences, but is not a binding contract. Your provider will do what is necessary at the time to keep you and your baby healthy and, though he or she will certainly consult with you, the plan is going to go out the window if there is an emergency or complication. Your birth plan is of most use to you, and although it can offer your health care provider information about your preferences, it is not a document he or she is going to keep close at hand during your labor and delivery.

Informed Consent

Whenever you receive medical care, you have the right to be completely informed about the treatment and any risks or possible outcomes. Make sure your health care provider discusses the potential effects and side effects of treatment choices not only for you but also for your baby. Your health care provider cannot hold back information because he or she doesn't want to upset you or because he or she knows what is best for you. You are the one who will be deciding what treatment you will accept, so you have the right to be completely informed.

Unfortunately, some health care providers find that they do not have the time to completely inform all patients about all risks or possible outcomes. No one sits you down and explains the benefits and risks to having blood drawn, for example. It's your job as a patient to ask questions and speak up when there are things that are new to you, that confuse you, or that are not clear to you. You should always ask for details about:

- **Medications.** Find out side effects, effect on the baby, and possible alternatives.
- **Invasive procedures.** Get details about anything that involves surgery, needles, or pelvic exams.
- **Problems you are experiencing.** Discuss pain, discomfort, reactions, and so on.
- **Tests.** Discuss the reason for the test, any risks, if there is any pain or discomfort involved, and alternatives.
- **Information.** Get any information that you feel has not been made completely clear to you.
- **Issues that frighten you or make you nervous.**

Second Opinions

There may come a time in your pregnancy when you feel you want a second opinion. A second opinion is a good idea when:

- Surgery or another radical treatment is recommended
- You cannot get a satisfactory answer or explanation
- You receive a diagnosis that is bad news or one you believe is wrong

- You begin to feel you cannot trust or respect your current health care provider
- You want information about alternative or nontraditional treatments
- A test that carries high risks is recommended
- You do not believe a test result
- Your concerns are not being listened to or responded to
- Your health care provider is hard to reach, unapproachable, or unfriendly

Your health insurance carrier will usually pay for a second opinion without a problem, although you may need to call to get clearance. To find a health care provider for a second opinion, do not ask your current provider! He or she will probably recommend someone that is likely to agree with the current diagnosis. Instead, ask family and friends or your primary doctor for names or check the list of participating health care providers in your area.

When seeking a second opinion:

- Choose someone from a different practice.
- Consider seeing a specialist if your concerns or issues warrant it (for example, if you have continued bleeding during pregnancy, see a perinatologist, a high-risk pregnancy specialist).
- When you call to make the appointment, explain that you want to come for a second opinion.
- Take copies of your medical records and test results with you to the appointment (you will need to call at least a week in advance to obtain these from your current health care provider and you may be required to pay a copying charge).
- Go armed with a list of questions and a notepad to write answers.
- Take someone with you so that you have help remembering everything you are told.

- If you like the second health care provider more, ask if he or she can take you on as a patient.
- Bring a list of all your current medications (or just bring the bottles with you).

Prenatal Testing

Prenatal testing is a part of pregnancy care that can be a bit nerve-racking but can help make certain risks clear and, at the very least, allow you to plan or consider the options that are available to you. According to the March of Dimes, approximately 250 types of birth defects can be detected with prenatal testing. Some tests are routine (done for all women), including:

- Blood tests for blood type, Rh factor, HIV, hepatitis B, syphilis, and rubella immunity
- Multiple marker screen (also called a quad marker screen)
- Urine analysis for preeclampsia and gestational diabetes
- Cervical tests for strep, gonorrhea, and chlamydia
- Ultrasounds
- Testing for gestational diabetes
- Blood pressure measurements at each appointment
- Measurement of fundal height (growth of your uterus) at each appointment
- Checking ankles for swelling
- Checking the baby's heartbeat

Other tests that are performed less routinely include:

- Chorionic villi sampling (CVS)
- Alpha-fetoprotein (AFP) screening
- Amniocentesis
- Nonstress tests
- Contraction stress test

These tests carry more risks than routine tests (or they have a high false-positive rate) and are often ordered only when a problem is suspected or when there are other risk factors present that need to be fully evaluated. Be sure to talk to your health care provider about these tests if they are recommended for you. The March of Dimes offers information about prenatal testing at: www.March ofDimes.com.

Whenever a nonroutine test is ordered, it is your right to ask for details about the purpose, risks, and procedure for the test. Ask the following questions:

- Why is this test being recommended?
- How exactly is the test performed?
- What discomfort, if any, will I experience?
- What information will this test provide?
- How soon can this test be scheduled?
- How soon will results be available?
- What are the potential risks this test poses? What are the statistics for those risks? Why do the benefits outweigh the risks?
- How accurate are the test results? Are there high false-positives or -negatives?
- If this were you, would you have the test?
- What kind of preparation is necessary for this test?
- How long does the test take?

As with any medical care, you have the right to refuse the test. If you are uncomfortable about the procedure, believe it is too risky, or believe that test results would not change your decision in any way, then turning down the test may be an option for you. Make sure you are fully informed before making the decision to refuse a test and always ask if there is a window of time in which you can change your mind about it (some tests can only be performed within a certain time period, while others are more flexible).

If a test reveals information that leads you to consider ending the pregnancy, talk to your health care provider about your options. To learn about your state laws and time frames in which you can consider this, visit: www.PlannedParenthood.org.

Understanding Medical Malpractice Laws

You may have all the confidence in the world in your health care provider, and it is most likely that he or she will provide you with excellent care. However, it's important to understand what your rights are should you not receive the kind of care you are expecting.

Medical malpractice is a legal term that refers to a medical care provider's legal responsibility when a mistake or unfortunate outcome occurs. However, a health care provider is not always responsible every time an unfortunate outcome takes place. Sometimes, there is nothing anyone could have done to prevent or change the result and no one is to blame. Other times, though, there were things the health care provider could or should have done that would have changed the result.

Medical malpractice happens when the doctor or other health care provider was negligent—which means he or she did not exercise the standard of care that the medical profession expects under similar circumstances. This means that he or she did not do what most health care providers would have done in the same situation. It also can mean that he or she did something other health care providers would not have done, or that he or she failed to ask for a test or other diagnostic tool that most other health care providers would have asked for.

Malpractice can occur at any stage of prenatal, delivery, or postpartum care. In order for there to be a malpractice claim, you must be able to show that the health care provider did something that caused the unfortunate outcome. Generally malpractice cases are worth pursuing only when the possible award is more than the cost of the legal action itself. If your doctor nicked you on the inside of the leg with her ring during an exam or if the midwife created a bruise on the baby's leg by holding too tightly during delivery, the resulting harm is minimal and it would not be worth pursuing.

If your health care provider should do something significant and cause an unfortunate outcome for you or your baby, you can take action. One option is a lawsuit. However, if you feel that it wouldn't make financial sense for you to pursue a lawsuit, you do still have the option of reporting the incident to the state medical board, which can take disciplinary action against the health care provider.

To find contact information for your state medical board, go to: www.fsmb.org/members.htm.

If you do decide you want to pursue a malpractice case, make sure you use an attorney who is experienced in medical malpractice. If you don't know an attorney who has this experience, your local or state bar association may have a referral program that can put you in touch with an attorney in your area. Most medical malpractice lawyers take the case on a contingency (usually one-third of the settlement or award), which means they don't get paid if they don't win the case for you. However, you are always responsible for paying for the expenses incurred during the preparation of the case—the experts, the court fees, copying, mail, etc.

Each state has a statute of limitations, a law that says how soon after an event you must begin to file papers. Normally you have about two years, which is usually adequate time to realize something went wrong and who was to blame. State statutes of limitations are available at: www.medical-malpractice.us.com/states.html.

Medical Leave for Miscarriage

Should a miscarriage happen to you, the first thing to be concerned with is taking care of your health, resting, healing, and coping. Pregnancy loss is a difficult thing to deal with, and most employers are very understanding and will give you the time you need to recover. Call in sick (or have your partner call for you) and figure out the details later.

Once you're over the initial shock, find out how many sick days or personal days you are allotted per year and how many you have used. Your doctor may be able to place you on disability (see Chapter 5) for a short period while you are recuperating, but you usually have to use your sick or personal time first.

You may also choose to consider taking an unpaid leave under the Family and Medical Leave Act (see Chapter 5) if you find you can't go back to work and you have used up all of your other time.

Help and support for pregnancy loss is available at: www
.nationalshareoffice.com.

Your Finances

Early Pregnancy Classes

You are probably familiar with childbirth classes, which women
take in their third trimester to help prepare them for labor. More
and more women are also signing up for early pregnancy classes.
These classes teach about body changes during pregnancy, pregnancy nutrition, and pregnancy exercise and also offer a support
element. You might also be interested in a more specific type of
class such as:

- Pregnancy Pilates
- Pregnancy yoga
- Pregnancy fitness
- Pregnancy nutrition
- Pregnancy after loss support

Contact your health insurance company to find out if you have
coverage for any of these classes. While many policies do not provide coverage, they may provide a discount if you attend a class
the company has partnered with, so be sure to ask for a list of participating classes.

Your Pregnancy Budget

Creating a pregnancy budget will help you take a look at the
expenses you have coming in the next seven months and will allow
you to create a savings plan for coping with those expenses, as well
as the expenses you will have once the baby is born.

Expenses are different for each woman and for each pregnancy.
If you have already had a child, you have much of what you will
need, so your expenses will be less. If you just got pregnant,

you can't possibly already know everything you're going to buy or how much it is all going to cost. Also, you'll probably receive many essentials as gifts. This budget is meant to be a work in progress, as well as a list of things you need to buy. Continue to update it throughout your pregnancy and make adjustments where necessary.

Focus on medical care costs and maternity items for now and gradually fill in the other items as your pregnancy progresses. Total the medical and maternity items and determine a monthly average (by dividing the total by seven—the months left in your pregnancy). This is the additional expense you will have each month. It can be helpful to create a separate total for big-ticket items such as cribs, car seats, strollers, and high chairs. You can save money separately for these items.

Once you know how much extra money you need, you may wish to begin placing money in a savings account each week so that you have money set aside just for these purposes. If your budget is already very tight, it's time for you to decide where you will make cuts in current expenses or how you will earn extra money. You can also consider ways to reduce your pregnancy expenses, such as borrowing maternity clothes from friends, buying used maternity clothes and baby furniture, or switching to an in-network care provider to lower your medical costs.

To estimate costs, talk to friends and family, shop online, or look at ads in your local paper. A rough price range for some items has been included in the worksheet on the next page to give you some idea of what things cost; however, this can vary widely depending on what brands you purchase or what bells and whistles you want, so be sure to do your homework and estimate a cost that will be real for you.

The worksheet includes some items you may not have thought of yet, which will be discussed in later chapters, so throughout this book you will be reminded to build on this budget as each month passes and as you make purchases or discover items you need to purchase. Approximate costs are included in parentheses to help you get a preliminary sense of the cost of items you may not be familiar with.

PREGNANCY BUDGET

Medical Care
Total amount of co-pays for office visits during pregnancy _____
Total deductibles _____
Expenses for nontraditional health care providers _____
Prescription costs _____
Cord blood collection kit ($1,200–$1,500) _____
Newborn blood testing kit ($90) _____
Additional ultrasound (not ordered by doctor) ($60–$150) _____

Maternity Items
Maternity clothing ($200–$2,000) _____
Shoes (if current ones should no longer fit or are not
  comfortable) ($40–$300) _____
Body pillow ($15–$50) _____
Pregnancy journal ($20) _____
Thank-you notes and postage for shower gifts ($15) ✗_____
Baby care books ($20–$50) _____
Special foods or Preggie Pops for cravings or morning
  sickness ($10–$200) _____

Classes and Education
Early pregnancy classes ($40–$100) _____
Prenatal classes ($40–$100) _____
Sibling classes ($10–$20) _____
Breastfeeding, CPR, or baby care classes ($20–$50) ✗_____
DVDs or videos ($14–$150) _____
Books ($12–$200) _____
Computer software ($15–$100) _____

Savings
Money into emergency fund (varies) _____

Baby Furniture and Large Items

You may not want or need to purchase all of these items. Fill in the amounts for the items you plan on purchasing.

Crib ($150–$2,000)   ?

Bassinet ($30–$300)   ✗

Changing table ($70–$500)   _____

Rocking chair ($100–$700)   _____

Car seat(s) ($75–$200)   ✗

Bouncer ($20–$80)   ✗

Exersaucer ($40–$100)   _____

Stroller ($100–$300)   ✗

Portable crib or playpen ($30–$100)   _____

Other items: _____   _____

Baby Supplies

Sling or carrier ($20–$100)   ✗

Room decor (varies)   _____

Diaper pail/disposal ($5–$50)   ✗

Clothing (varies)   ✗

Diaper bag ($15–$100)   ✗

Diapers for first weeks ($20–$60)   ✗

Wipes for first weeks ($10–$20)   ✗

Baby bathtub and skin care products ($30–$70)   ✗

Bedding ($30–$400)   ✗

Breast pump ($40–$500)   ✗

Nursing pads, bras, clothes, and pillows ($30–$200)   ✗

Bibs, burp cloths, and feeding supplies ($40–$200)   ✗

Mobile ($15–$80)   ✗

Toys and books (varies)   _____

Pacifiers, bottles, nipples, and bottle-cleaning
   supplies ($20–$100)   ✗

Lanolin (for sore nipples) ($3–$10)   ✗

Babyproofing supplies ($20–$200)   _____

Home testing ($30–$500)   _____

Baby monitor ($30–$200) ____

Thermometer ($5–$100) ~~____~~

Other

_____ ____

_____ ____

_____ ____

_____ ____

_____ ____

TOTAL ____

WEEKLY AMOUNT (divide total by the number of
weeks left in your pregnancy) ____

The weekly amount is the money you need to save per week to
manage all of your costs. The best plan is to try to save this amount
from the beginning. Once you have a baby shower and people start
giving you secondhand items, you will be able to significantly
reduce the amount of items you will need to buy. But you should
still try to save this amount of money and put it in a savings
account, or once your baby is born you can place it in a college
savings plan.

46
...

Your Lifestyle

Meeting Up with Other Moms

This is a great time to go online and join some birth month
groups—message boards or discussion groups where moms who
are due in the same month can meet, talk about what they are
going through, offer support, commiserate, and get to know each
other. When you talk to other women who are experiencing the

same things you are, you will get not only support but also ideas. If you are having trouble coping with morning sickness, are making decisions about prenatal testing, or are wondering if your health care provider is right for you, you can find other women who are sharing your exact concerns and may be able to share solutions with you. You will also feel less alone if you can talk to other people who are experiencing the same things you are. Many of these groups last beyond the pregnancies and go on to become close friends. You can find birth month groups at:

- http://bbs.babycenter.com/boards/bbs-birthclubs
- www.epregnancy.com/messagebrd/index.php
- http://talk.thebabycorner.com/forumdisplay.php?f=120
- www.parentsplace.com

Subscribing to Pregnancy and Baby Magazines

There are many magazines available for expectant parents today. The magazines can keep you up-to-date on changes in medical recommendations and offer support and information as you go through your pregnancy.

Every Baby magazine is available free at midwifery practices. Some magazines are free by mail or at maternity stores:

- *American Baby* (www.AmericanBaby.com)
- *Baby Talk* (www.BabyTalk.com)

Other magazines are subscription only, including:

- *ePregnancy* (www.ePregnancy.com)
- *Pregnancy* (www.PregnancyMagazine.com)
- *Fit Pregnancy* (www.FitPregnancy.com)

If you want to consider one of the many pregnancy and baby magazines, pick up a copy at your library or buy an issue at the grocery store or bookstore before subscribing.

Coping with Morning Sickness

If you're experiencing morning sickness, it's important to talk with your health care provider about your specific situation and what you can do to ease it and stay healthy. To cope, the American Pregnancy Association recommends that you:

- Eat small, frequent meals
- Drink and eat at separate times
- Eat small crackers, such as oyster crackers, and try nibbling them before getting out of bed
- Drink ginger tea or eat ginger snaps
- Eat or sniff lemons
- Avoid napping right after eating
- Eat bland foods
- Listen to your cravings
- Avoid being in overly warm places
- Try seasickness or morning sickness wristbands
- Discuss vitamin B_6 with your health care provider
- Drink enough fluids
- Try Preggie Pops—lollipops designed to help ease nausea (www.preggiepops.com)
- Avoid eating spicy or greasy food at night
- Get enough sleep

For more help with morning sickness, see: www.SOSmorningsickness.com.

Books About Morning Sickness

The Morning Sickness Companion by Elizabeth Kaledin (St. Martin's Griffin, 2003, $14.95).

Managing Morning Sickness by Miriam Erick (Bull Publishing, 2004, $16.95).

If you're finding that morning sickness is impacting your ability to work, talk to your employer. Find out if you can change your hours so you can come into work later and stay later. If there is a smell in your workplace that is making you sick, talk about whether it can be removed or whether you could work in another area. Try to take short, frequent breaks instead of longer ones— discuss this with your employer if you think it might be a problem. Stress that you want to continue working but need some small changes to make it manageable for you.

Although you can ask your employer to be understanding, your rights are the same as they are when you have any other illness. You can use your sick time and try to manage as best you can, but once your sick time is gone you're left with the choice of getting through somehow or taking leave as per the Family and Medical Leave Act (FMLA; see Chapter 5). If you are absent and have used your sick time and have not applied for or do not qualify for FMLA, your employer can fire you. If you're able to get to work but the quality of your work is suffering because you are distracted or not feeling well, the best plan is to talk with your supervisor. Find ways to make up for the quality of your work, such as offering to take some work home or swap tasks with someone else. Female coworkers are likely to be sympathetic to your plight and may be willing to help you out.

Exercise

Whether or not you exercised regularly prior to your pregnancy, it is important to remain active during your pregnancy. However, check with your health care provider before exercising during pregnancy. The American Pregnancy Association recommends that you do the following:

- Start a new exercise program slowly (and only after consulting your health care provider).
- Be attuned to the signals your body gives you.

- Avoid exercising to the point of exhaustion or shortness of breath.
- Wear appropriate exercise shoes.
- Drink plenty of fluids while exercising.
- Take frequent breaks.
- Avoid exercising in very hot weather.
- Avoid contact sports.
- Avoid lifting weights over your head or using weights that strain your lower back.
- Avoid any exercise for which you lie flat on your back.
- Be sure to stretch before and after exercising.

Pregnancy Exercise Videos/DVDs

Leisa Hart's Fit Mama (Goldhill Home Media I, 2003, DVD: $19.95, VHS: $14.98).

Prenatal Pilates (Pilates Pregnancy, 2003, DVD: $21.99, VHS: $19.95).

Crunch Yoga Mama: Prenatal Yoga (Anchor Bay Entertainment, 2003, DVD: $21.95, VHS: $14.99).

Quick Fix Prenatal Workout (Inspired Corporation, 2003, DVD: $14.98, VHS: $9.98).

Computerizing Your Pregnancy

There are a variety of software programs that can be helpful during your pregnancy and can help you stay organized or focused on your diet.

- **Baby Progress:** This free program helps you track your baby's gestational age and the number of days until your due date. Find it at: www.babiesonline.com/BabyProgress.
- **Nutrigenie Pregnancy Nutrition:** This $39 program helps you create a weight gain plan and analyzes your diet, identifying

the number of calories, fats, carbs, and nutrients in your diet. The program can also generate menus for you to follow and can be used to help you lose weight after the baby is born. Find it at: http://nutri genie.biz/ngpn41.html.

• **Mom to Be:** This $35 program allows you to keep a daily journal, create lists, and input photos or video. You can generate reports from your journal that you can send to friends and relatives. It also includes the Chinese Baby Sex Calculator.

• **HeyBaby:** This free program is for a pocket PC or Palm OS and allows you to track your baby's development and growth, choose names, look up pregnancy terms in a glossary, and calculate ovulation. Find it at: www.programurl.com/software/preg nancy.htm.

Month 2 Checklist
☐ Begin to think about creating a birth plan.
☐ Read and learn about any prenatal tests that have been or might be ordered for you.
☐ Consider signing up for early pregnancy classes.
☐ Create a pregnancy budget.
☐ Check out due date clubs and think about joining one.
☐ Subscribe to pregnancy and baby magazines.
☐ Talk to your health care provider about morning sickness, if you are experiencing it.
☐ Consider purchasing pregnancy exercise videos or DVDs.
☐ Consider purchasing a pregnancy software program.

4

Month 3

*A*pril loved her job as a pediatric nurse. She was in her third
month of pregnancy and now suddenly seemed to be coming down with every bug that walked in the door at work. Her
midwife assured her it wasn't going to hurt the baby, and if she
wanted to continue to work, she should. Her supervisor had a different idea and wanted to move her to a job just answering
phones. She wondered if her supervisor could require her to do
this and what would happen if she refused. Because of this and
other reasons, April was considering looking for a job elsewhere,

By the time you're into month three of your pregnancy you're
probably already revealing or thinking about revealing your
happy news to friends and coworkers. After all, you're practically
bursting with the news and can probably no longer contain
yourself. During this month, you'll need to deal with
"coming out" as an expectant parent at work. It's also
time to take a closer look at your birth plan and
budget (which you've thought carefully about in
previous months).

but she wondered if she would have to tell the new employer that she was pregnant and if that meant she would not be hired.

Your Rights

Your Job

Your pregnancy doesn't have to affect your job. Many women are able to continue working right to the very end. However, if your job involves heavy lifting or a lot of standing or walking, you may get to the point near the end of your pregnancy when you become uncomfortable. Before making any decisions about how long you'll continue working or if you need a change in job responsibilities, understand your rights and protections.

Telling Your Employer About Your Pregnancy

Many women wait until they are showing to let a supervisor know. It's your choice when you want to share your news. If you tell coworkers or friends, though, you should tell your supervisor at the same time because word will get around. When you tell your supervisor you are pregnant, you do not need to have a complete plan for how much time you want to take off when the baby is born. Simply share the news and if you are asked, say you haven't yet decided how much time you want or need.

If your company has on-site day care and you think you might be interested in using it, get on the waiting list now to reserve a space. In large companies there can be long waiting lists.

Pregnancy Discrimination

You have an absolute right to work while you are pregnant. The federal Pregnancy Discrimination Act of 1978 (PDA) applies to employers with fifteen or more employees and says an employer can't refuse to hire or promote you and can't fire you just because you're pregnant. Despite the law, you may notice that subtle discrimination occurs. For example, you might be passed over for a promotion and you may believe it was because you're pregnant. (This is often the beginning of the "mommy track"—subtle differences in the way working mothers are treated that impacts their ability to get promoted, earn more, or achieve more at work.) Or you might not get a job you interview for and believe it is because you're obviously pregnant. The problem is that if something like this does happen, it can be difficult to prove that the decisions made were based on your being pregnant. If you do have suspicions, report them to the federal Equal Employment Opportunity Commission, whether or not you think you can prove it, since it is always a good idea to report possible breaches—even if nothing is done in your case, it could mean other women's complaints are taken seriously. You can file pregnancy discrimination complaints at: www.eeoc.gov/charge/overview_charge_filing.html.

If you're worried about being "mommy tracked," start thinking about steps you can take to prevent it from happening. This may mean taking on more responsibility or initiative, being more aggressive at work, and planning for work you will handle after the baby arrives so that your employer knows that your job is and will always be a priority.

Your employer can't require you to take a mandatory leave while pregnant or after the baby is born (in the past, employers had policies of putting women on leave once they began to show). If you wish to work during your pregnancy (and right up to the birth), you must be allowed to do so. If you take a leave or go on disability during your pregnancy (for health problems) and then become able to return to work when your condition improves, your employer must allow you to return if you choose to.

Under the Pregnancy Discrimination Act, your employer must provide you with the same treatment as other employees with medical conditions. So, for example, if your employer has allowed a sick coworker to regularly leave early for doctor appointments, you must be given the same treatment. But if your employer has a policy of firing people for excessive absences or tardiness, then you can be fired if you're routinely late because of morning sickness or you take a lot of days off when you're not feeling well.

Asking for Changes in Job Responsibility

The Supreme Court has ruled that women are the only ones who can make decisions about risks to their unborn babies while working. This means your employer cannot remove you from a position he or she feels is "dangerous" because you are pregnant. If your job involves things like exposure to chemicals, radiation, loud noises, extreme temperatures, smoke, or other conditions that could be harmful to you or your baby, you should discuss the work conditions with your health care provider and decide if it is safe for you to continue. Your employer cannot require you to leave your position—it must be your decision. If you work in a job in which you are exposed to dangerous conditions, your employer might require you to sign a waiver, relieving the company of responsibility if you choose to continue working in the environment.

If you decide it's unsafe or too uncomfortable for you to continue doing your job while pregnant and your health care provider agrees, your employer must give you different tasks or allow you to take a disability leave or a leave without pay (see Chapter 5 for more information about this). The best way to go about getting a change in job responsibilities is to talk with your supervisor and explain why you feel it's unsafe to continue with your current job tasks or assignments. You'll want to make it clear that you want to keep your job and plan to continue working, but that you just don't feel you can continue with the same tasks. Some employers will be very flexible, while others will require a written letter from your health care provider and will generate a lot of paperwork and procedures. You may also need to speak to your union representative (if you have one) or your human resources manager, but it's often a good idea to let your supervisor know personally, since he or she will be more likely to feel sympathetic toward you if you make this a human issue and not a paperwork one.

For assistance with work and pregnancy issues, contact:

Women, Work! The National Network for Women's Employment
202-467-6346
www.womenwork.org

Interviewing for a New Job

If you interview for a new job while pregnant, you're not required to tell the employer you are pregnant and he or she cannot ask you if you are, if you have children, or if you plan to have children. Note that you would not be eligible for a leave under the Family Medical Leave Act (FMLA, see Chapter 5) until you have worked at your job for twelve months. A new employer cannot deny you health insurance because you are pregnant.

Thinking About Staying Home

If you currently work, you may be considering stay-at-home motherhood. How will leaving your job affect your family's finances? Can you survive financially without your income? Are there ways you can earn money and stay home at the same time? Think about steps you need to take to make this a reality. Take a look at your budget and see what you can cut to compensate for the loss of your income. Try using this online calculator to help you make the stay-at-home decision: www.kiplinger.com/tools/managing/afford.html.

While staying at home does mean a reduction in your income, it also means some substantial savings. Take into consideration the following savings:

- Work clothes and shoes
- Business expenses (appointment books, briefcases, office parties, work social events, office gifts)
- Transportation to and from work (gas, tolls, parking, car maintenance, or public transportation)
- Day care for your baby
- Lunches, coffee, and other food you buy while at work
- Things you will have more time for (such as cooking more, washing your own car, shopping for bargains)

For information about staying home with your baby see:

- Family and Home Network (www.familyandhome.org)
- National Association of At-Home Mothers (www.athome mothers.com)

STAY-AT-HOME WORKSHEET

Describe how you will adjust your budget to compensate for your loss of income (see later in this chapter for a list of expenses you may be able to cut out of your budget): _____

_____

_____

_____

How will staying home with your baby affect your self-image? Some women find that losing touch with coworkers can be difficult and isolating. How will you find support and friendship while staying home with your baby? _____

_____

_____

_____

Are you prepared to take on the burden of being the primary caregiver for your child? Many women envision parenthood as a partnership, but if your partner is going off to work every day and you are home alone with the baby, it can quickly begin to feel like an unequal balance. How will you feel being the parent who provides most of the child care? _____

_____

_____

_____

Do you feel sad about leaving your job? Does leaving your job somehow make you feel diminished or less important? Are you uncomfortable relying completely on your partner for financial support? How will you work through these feelings and overcome them? _____

_____

_____

If you choose to become a stay-at-home mom, expect to find that there is a real transition period. You won't adjust right away, and if you are leaving your job around the time your baby is being born, you will have two major life changes taking place at the same time. To make stay-at-home motherhood work, make sure you:

- **Make time for yourself.** It's hard to do but you need to plan time for youself, to keep your sanity.
- **Make time for your partner.** It's important that you continue to have time for each other.
- **Make time for things that matter to you.** Continue to do things that make you feel useful and intelligent, such as a hobby and spending time with friends.
- **Set realistic goals for yourself.** Just because you are now staying home, you can't expect yourself to have a perfectly clean home, cook gourmet meals, or exercise every day.
- **Find ways to keep costs down.** There's nothing worse than feeling like you are trapped in the house with the baby and have no money to do anything. Find inexpensive ways to have fun and trim the unneeded extras out of your life.
- **Keep the right mindset.** Stay-at-home moms do an important, worthwhile job. You're not just staying home; you're raising a human being.

Books for At-Home Moms

The Stay-at-Home Parent's Survival Guide by Christina Baglivi Tinglof (McGraw-Hill, 2000, $14.95).

Staying Home: From Full-Time Professional to Full-Time Parent by Darcie Sanders (Spencer & Waters, 2001, $14.95).

You Can Afford to Stay Home with Your Kids: A Step-by-Step Guide for Converting Your Family from Two Incomes to One by Malia McCawley Wyckoff (Career Press, 1999, $14.95).

Mr. Mom

If you can't or don't want to stay home with your baby, another option is for your spouse to do so. The number of at-home fathers is growing, and it may make the most sense if your income is higher or if you just don't think you would enjoy being home with your child full-time. When considering this option:

- Think how you will feel about being the primary earner in the family.
- Give some thought as to how you feel about having Dad provide care full-time.
- Talk with your spouse about how this decision will change and impact his life and career path.
- Consider whether your health insurance policy is adequate for your family's needs.
- Think about whether you will be breastfeeding and how you will make arrangements for this.

For help and support with at-home fatherhood, contact:

- www.Fatherhood.org
- www.Slowlane.com
- www.Daddyshome.org
- www.Fathers.com

Books for At-Home Dads

The Stay-at-Home Dad Handbook by Peter Baylies (Chicago Review Press, 2004, $14.95).

Stay-at-Home Dads: The Essential Guide to Creating the New Family by Libby Gill (Plume Books, 2001, $14.00).

Pregnancy and Divorce

If you are married and your relationship is over, or you're worried that it might be, it's important to understand the facts about divorce. If you divorce while you are pregnant, nothing about custody or child support can be decided until after the baby is born. Once the baby is born, you or your spouse (or ex if your divorce is final by then) would need to file papers to ask the court to determine custody and child support. At one time there was a presumption in the law that young children should automatically live with their mothers, but this is no longer the case. Custody is decided based on the best interests of the child. This usually means that the child will have one primary home with one parent and spend occasional time with the other parent.

The parent with whom the child lives most of the time is entitled to child support. Child support is calculated as a percent of income, usually 17 percent.

For more information about divorce see:

- **State divorce laws:** www.findlaw.com
- **State child support calculators:** www.alllaw.com/calculators/childsupport

If you are considering divorce, you might want to consider mediation as an alternative to a courtroom divorce. A mediator is a neutral third party (usually a lawyer or therapist) who helps you and your spouse create a settlement yourselves. For information or to find a mediator in your area, contact the Association for Conflict Resolution at 202-464-9700, or www.acresolution.org.

Finding Out Your Baby's Sex

With the various tests you will likely have, you may have the option of finding out your baby's sex. Some parents like to get this information since it makes buying clothes and decorating the nursery easier. Others prefer the element of surprise. Discuss this decision with your partner.

Since the baby's sex is part of your medical information, it is information you have the right to access; your health care provider must share this information with you if you want it. If you don't want to find out, you can ask that you not be told. If you want to know and your partner doesn't, or vice versa, you can specify this. Most health care providers pay little attention to the sex of the baby unless there is a medical reason (such as a history of sex-linked genetic disorders). Should someone slip up and tell you when you don't want to know, you don't have any recourse.

A study published in the journal *Ultrasound in Obstetrics & Gynecology* tested the accuracy of ultrasound sex determinations. At eleven weeks predictions were correct 46 percent of the time, at twelve weeks 75 percent, at thirteen weeks 79 percent, and at fourteen weeks 90 percent. Amniocentesis is 99 percent accurate (and inaccurate only when the sample is too small).

Asking for Extra Tests

Some parents ask their health care providers to perform additional ultrasounds or other tests, beyond what is normally ordered. You can always ask, but your health care provider will order only those tests he or she finds to be medically necessary and your health insurance will pay only for those that your health care provider orders.

There has been a huge growth in businesses that will do ultra-sounds during pregnancy without a doctor's order, as long as the parents pick up the cost. Some health care providers believe it is not safe to have more ultrasounds than are medically necessary, though others see no harm in it. These businesses charge between $60 and $150 to do an ultrasound and provide you with a video or DVD of the scan. If this is something you are interested in doing, check with your health care provider.

Your Finances

Pregnancy and Debt

If you're like a lot of people, you have some debt—maybe student loans, credit card debt, car loans, or a mortgage. Now that you're going to be a parent, you're probably starting to think about some long-term issues, like:

- How am I going to pay for my child's college education?
- How will we afford a home that is big enough for all of us?
- How can we afford all of the purchases we need to make?

Because pregnancy is a turning point in your life, this is a good time to rethink your attitude about debt. If you are carrying a lot of debt, now may be the time to consider how you can reduce it. You know that you have big expenses coming in the future, but it's difficult to consider dealing with those when you're overwhelmed with debt today. Use these strategies to reduce your current debt:

- **Make payments, no matter how small.** If you have credit card debt or an overdue student loan, it may seem simply overwhelming because it is so large. But the truth is, if you don't start paying it off now in small amounts, you're going to be buried in interest later. Do what you can to start paying these debts down.
- **Refinance.** If you have student loans, look into a consolidation loan that may offer a better interest rate or more reasonable monthly payments. Transferring balances on credit cards can net you lower interest rates. Taking out a home equity loan can allow you to pay off other debt while deducting the home equity interest on your taxes.
- **Get tough on spending.** Don't spend more than you have. Period. Cut up your credit cards or stick them in the freezer so you have them only for emergencies. Stop adding to your debt.
- **Negotiate.** If you have a large amount of credit card debt, negotiate with the company. It is possible to negotiate a payoff that is less than the full amount owed, since the company would rather get 80 percent of the debt in cash today than spend three years chasing you down to get 100 percent.

This is a good time to take stock of the debt you have, so that as you face the new expenses you will be incurring you will have a handle on your real financial picture. When you apply for credit, creditors look at your debt-to-income ratio. They divide the amounts you pay monthly on debt (credit card debt, student loans, mortgages, etc.) by your monthly income. A ratio of 10 percent or less is ideal. Between 10 percent and 20 percent is a concern, and higher than that is a red flag. A high ratio doesn't mean you won't be able to get credit (credit card companies love to collect interest when you can't pay off your debt), but it could impact your ability to get a mortgage, not to mention that it is a sign that you need to reduce your debt so that you can live more affordably. Use the debt worksheet below to get a grip on your current debt.

If you are unsure about balances, call and ask. You should also obtain a copy of your credit report. A credit report is a complete

DEBT WORKSHEET

Name of Creditor	Account Number	Monthly Payment	Balance
_____	_____	_____	_____
_____	_____	_____	_____
_____	_____	_____	_____
_____	_____	_____	_____
_____	_____	_____	_____
_____	_____	_____	_____
_____	_____	_____	_____
_____	_____	_____	_____
_____	_____	_____	_____

listing of all the debt you have. It's important to obtain this, because there may be old debts you have forgotten about that are negatively affecting your credit rating. There are three major credit reporting companies, and it is a good idea to obtain a report for you and your spouse (if you are married, since you each have separate reports, even though you may have some joint debt) or partner from each of the three. They may each have different information (because different creditors report their information to different companies). If you have been denied credit, you are entitled to a free report. Beginning in the fall of 2005, each person will be entitled to one free report from each company every twelve months.

Credit Reporting Agencies
Equifax
800-685-1111
www.equifax.com

Experian
888-397-3742
www.experian.com

TransUnion
800-888-4213
www.tuc.com

You can get a free annual report at:
www.annualcreditreport.com
877-322-8228

Your credit report may also show accounts that are open, with no balance on them. If these are accounts you no longer use, write to the creditor and have the accounts closed. Even though they may have no current balance, you still have credit available there and this may cut down on your ability to obtain new credit.

In general, pregnancy is not a good time to incur new debt. Your family is about to undergo a fundamental change. Even if you think you are going to go back to work after the baby arrives, you may find that your decision could change once the baby is born. This is a time in your life when you have a lot of important decisions ahead of you. It's best to try to reduce your existing debt and keep new debt to an absolute minimum right now because you don't really know where you will be financially in eight or nine months.

To be smart about using debt:

• **Use free financing.** Offers like 0 percent for twelve months by store credit cards can be a good deal, if you pay off the balance before the time period ends. Divide the total balance by the number of months the offer is good and make that payment each month.

• **Use credit as a convenience.** It can be hard to always have enough cash on hand to pay for the groceries, the bag of diapers you need to pick up, and the dirt-cheap baby clothes you find on clearance. Use credit cards as a way of making your life easy, but not as a way to rack up debt. Resolve to pay off your balance every single month and never ever leave it unpaid.

• **Remember that some debt is good.** When considering whether or not to go into debt, consider the benefit the debt offers you. A mortgage or a car loan is a good debt because you get something of great importance from these loans—a car or home you would be unable to afford any other way. But make sure that you can fit the monthly payments into your family's budget without squeezing.

Saving Money During Your Pregnancy

There's no question when you look at your pregnancy budget that having a baby can be quite expensive. Using your pregnancy budget and savings plan, you will be able to plan for these expenses and not be taken by surprise. However, there are ways to save money and cut your expenses that you may not have considered as you were drawing up your budget.

Vitamins

Although your health care provider may give you a prescription for prenatal vitamins, it might be cheaper for you to buy over-the-counter prenatal vitamins. Compare prices before purchasing. Your prescription drug plan may offer discounts for joining a mail club, where the prescriptions are delivered right to your door and are significantly less than the cost of traditional pharmacies. You may also be able to get a better price online. Check these online drugstores:

- www.drugstore.com
- www.PeopleRx.com

Diapers and Wipes

In a few months you will probably start laying in a supply of these items. Start looking at coupons now, and if they don't expire too soon, cut them out and save them. Get on mailing lists for the companies that make these items. Sign up for special baby club sale flyers that contain coupons at retailers like Kmart and Toys R Us.

Check the websites for diaper companies for special coupons and newsletters:

- www.Huggies.com
- www.Pampers.com
- www.Luvs.com

It's tempting to stock up on these items in advance as you see sales on them, but be aware that one brand of diapers might not fit your baby well, you might decide one brand of wipes is too thin, or your baby might outgrow one size of diapers quickly, leaving you with a stockpile you can't use. If you see a good deal, buy some but not a lot. Buy only a few bags of newborn-size diapers. If your baby is on the large side, they won't fit for long.

Baby Equipment

The furniture and equipment that you'll be purchasing for your baby can be quite expensive (as you probably noted when you drew up your budget!). However, there are many ways to save money on these items. If there is a holiday or birthday (for you or your partner) coming up before your due date, ask for some of these items as gifts. Remember also that you may receive some of them as shower gifts.

Start to ask friends and relatives about items you can borrow. Keep your eyes open for sales, clearances, yard sales, and items you come across at secondhand stores. You might find infant and toddler books at library sales. Haunt the end-of-season clearance racks at stores, but keep in mind how old your baby will be in each coming season and buy clothes that will be the right size for that season. Go to store closing sales and snap up bargains there. Ask about buying floor model cribs, strollers, and car seats at a discount. If you purchase items this way, be sure to update your budget to reflect your purchases.

Your Lifestyle

Staying Comfortable at Work

Remaining comfortable at work will help make your time there more pleasant and enable you to work as long as possible. Make sure you're using a chair that is adjustable and has armrests and lumbar support. If you experience back pain, bring a small pillow to work with you. A small footstool under your desk can help relieve leg pain or ankle swelling. Ask if your employer can provide these items; you may need to bring in a note from your health care provider explaining why you need them. If you sit a lot at work, make sure you stand up and stretch and move about often. Or if you stand or move about often during your job, take frequent short breaks and sit down. Make sure you drink enough fluids during the day and keep small snacks handy.

Maternity Clothes

Although you probably do not need maternity clothes yet, you will in the coming months. You may be able to continue to wear some items you currently own, like big sleep shirts or loose sweaters, so don't assume you have to replace everything. Borrowing maternity clothes from friends and family will cut costs. Secondhand or consignment shops are also good alternatives to spending a lot on maternity clothes. Maternity departments in discount stores are a good place to buy basics like hose, T-shirts, and turtlenecks. Many women shop at plus-size stores or departments and find that clothing a few sizes larger is comfortable and less expensive than maternity clothes.

To make your regular clothing last longer, purchase bra and waistband expanders. Purchase them online at: www.kidssurplus .com, or at local maternity shops or sewing supply stores.

Month 3 Checklist

☐ Decide when you want to tell your employer about your pregnancy.

☐ Get on the on-site day care waiting list if you are interested in this service.

☐ Consider work restrictions or changes if necessary and obtain a note from your health care provider if necessary.

☐ Think about stay-at-home parenthood options and complete the worksheet.

☐ Decide if you want to know your baby's sex.

☐ Complete the debt worksheet.

☐ Order credit reports.

☐ Compare vitamin prices.

☐ Sign up for free newsletters from diaper companies and look for coupons.

☐ Begin buying or borrowing maternity clothes.

5

Month 4

Karen was in her fourth month and was having some complications. Her doctor wanted her on bed rest for a few weeks. She called her human resources contact and learned that she qualified for state disability insurance, so that she would be paid a percent of her salary while she was out. She had her doctor complete the necessary paperwork. While she was ill, her husband lost his job. If she had not applied for disability insurance benefits, they would have had no income while she was not working.

As your belly begins to grow, you know that your pregnancy is moving along and that sooner than you can believe, your child will be here. As you enter the second trimester, you probably are starting to feel better—more energetic and less nauseous. It's time to harness that energy you are regaining and use it in the next couple of months to get things organized and ready.

Your Rights

Your Right to Refuse Medical Treatment

As you move further into your pregnancy, you may be confronted with a choice about tests, such as amniocentesis, and you may be starting to think about possible procedures during labor and delivery, such as fetal monitoring and episiotomies. You have the right to refuse any treatment, unless refusing the treatment endangers the life of your child, such as trying to get up and leave the hospital during surgery. Most of the time, your health care provider will offer you good advice, but sometimes women must decide on their own what is right for them and their babies. Remember that you have the absolute right to say no or to request more information before consenting to any procedure or treatment.

You can choose to check yourself out of any hospital, birth center, or facility. If you leave against the advice of your health care provider, it is called leaving AMA (against medical advice). Although you are in control of your body and your treatment, understand that if you leave AMA, your insurance company can refuse to pay for any later treatment that directly results from your leaving (such as developing an infection or needing an ambulance).

If your health care provider suggests a treatment or procedure you do not want, the best advice is to get more advice. Get a second or third opinion. Ask about options and alternatives.

Guardianship

Part of being a parent means planning for things that hopefully will never happen, so you must confront your own mortality and think about who you would want to care for your baby if you and your partner died. Many people mistakenly believe that by choosing godparents for their child, they have taken care of this problem. While godparents can play an important and meaningful role in a child's life, they have no legal right to care for your child should you die.

To make sure your bases are covered and your child will be safe and secure, have a will drawn up and name a guardian for your child soon after you give birth. Start thinking now about whom you will choose, as this can take some time and thought. The guardian can be anyone you choose but should be someone who:

- Has a relationship with your child
- Shares similar views with you
- Agrees to take on the responsibility
- Is a stable and trustworthy person
- Has a lifestyle conducive to raising children
- Welcomes the responsibility

After your baby is born, your attorney will draw up a will that allows you to designate a guardian and may also allow you to select an alternate, in case your first-choice person is unable to take on the responsibility for some reason. Some attorneys will do this before your baby is born, so be sure to ask if this is something you need to wait to take care of.

You may also be able to appoint someone other than the guardian to manage your child's finances, normally referred to as a financial guardian. Often, though, it makes sense to name the same person to do both jobs, since the person caring for the child will have a better sense as to what the child's needs are. See Chapter 6 for tips about approaching potential guardians.

Leave During Pregnancy

Most women have healthy pregnancies and are able to continue working until delivery. But some women are not able to work all the way through their pregnancies. It's important to think about your pregnancy-leave options now, so that you are prepared to make a decision if you are put on bed rest or have some other complication during pregnancy that requires you to take time off of work.

Disability Leave

Disability leave pays a percentage of your regular previous pay. Only California, Hawaii, New Jersey, New York, and Rhode Island have state disability programs that are mandatory. Each of these states has its own laws about state disability benefits, but generally you are considered "disabled" if you are medically unable to perform one or more of your job duties. So if you are on bed rest, hospitalized, or are told to stay off your feet completely, you would be unable to do your job. You do not need to use vacation time first. Disability leave kicks in once a doctor certifies you are disabled and you are past your state's waiting period (which is normally a few days).

Many companies have their own private disability insurance policies. Ask your human resources contact if your company has such a policy and what its requirements are. If your doctor certifies that you are unable to continue working due to a pregnancy-related condition, you can use your company's disability policy.

Your condition must be treated by your employer in the same manner in which other conditions are treated (this is governed by the Pregnancy Discrimination Act; see Chapter 4 for more information). So, if your employer offers paid leave for other medical conditions—anything from heart disease to a broken leg—he or she must provide paid leave for pregnancy complications. If your company has an official policy but has bent the rules in the past for other people with any kind of disability (for example, allowed employees with cancer to take extended leaves), then the rules must be bent for you. To prove that this happened you would need to talk to other employees and bring it to the attention of your human resources department. It can be difficult to prove.

If your rights are violated, contact your state attorney general's office or the Equal Employment Opportunity Commission (www .eeoc.gov).

Family and Medical Leave Act

The federal Family and Medical Leave Act (FMLA)—a federal law that was passed to allow people to take unpaid time off from work for illness or to care for family members while ensuring their jobs would still be there for them when they return—applies to you if you work for a public agency (federal, state, or local) or for a private employer with fifty or more employees, and if you have been employed there at least twelve months and worked at least 1,250 hours in the last twelve months.

You may take up to twelve weeks of unpaid leave in a twelve-month period for pregnancy or to care for a newborn. You don't need to provide medical documentation; you simply notify your employer that you are exercising your right to take this type of leave and you may need to sign some forms indicating that you are exercising this right. You can take this time off as one big block, or you can take it in pieces. For example, you might choose to work part-time during your last month of pregnancy. Remember that any time you take off during your pregnancy counts as part of your total twelve-week allowance per calendar year, so make sure you are also starting to think about how much time you would like to take off once the baby is born, if your due date is in the same calendar year.

Under FMLA your employer must keep your health benefits in place (but you may have to pay premiums yourself) while you are gone and must restore you to your original job or to an equivalent job with equivalent pay when you return. Your employer cannot penalize you for taking the leave or allow it to affect any of your benefits.

If you have vacation or sick time, you can choose to use this time in addition to the other time off, if you have accrued it and if you give the required amount of notice. You can be required to use paid vacation time concurrently or prior to your unpaid leave time. If your leave overlaps calendar years, make sure your employer does not require you to use vacation or sick time first in the new year before continuing with FMLA or state pregnancy leave time.

Individual states also have their own pregnancy leave acts, similar to the FMLA. States with family leave laws include:

- California
- Connecticut

- Hawaii
- Maine
- Minnesota
- New Jersey
- Oregon
- Rhode Island
- Vermont
- Washington
- Washington, DC
- Wisconsin

State family leave can be combined with federal FMLA leave to take a larger amount of time off.

For details on your state's family leave law, visit: www.dol.gov/esa/programs/whd/state/fmla.

To read the federal Family and Medical Leave Act, go to: www.dol.gov/esa/whd/fmla.

Smaller Companies and Self-Employment

If you are employed by a company with fewer than fifty employees, you are not covered by federal FMLA (check your state's laws to find out if you are covered by state family leave laws). If you're in this situation, find out if your company has a policy about pregnancy leaves and also determine what your state and municipal laws are, since these will determine what kind of disability leave you qualify for. Start with your human resources contact. If you cannot get help that way, call your state attorney general's office. See page 56 for contact information for an organization that helps working women.

If you are self-employed, you don't qualify for state disability payments. You can take out a private disability insurance policy; however, you must obtain this policy before becoming pregnant (see Chapter 1 for more information). Many women combine disability, vacation time, sick leave, state leave time, and FMLA when taking a leave during pregnancy. For tips on combining leaves, see Chapter 8.

Your Finances

Creating a Financial Cushion

By now you should be adjusting your pregnancy budget whenever you come across a new expense. But being prepared means more than having enough money to buy a crib. It also means you need to step back and prepare for any unexpected circumstances. For example, if you or your partner lose your job after your baby is born, you would need a financial cushion to help you survive. A financial cushion is important for unexpected medical costs, unexpected expenses, unplanned changes in your living arrangement, reductions in salaries, and so on. When you have a baby, there can be lots of unplanned expenses, such as sick visits to the doctor. If you or your partner plan on changing your employment status after the birth, start setting money aside now to help cushion the blow of losing or reducing one income.

To create a financial cushion, open a separate savings account and deposit a fixed amount into it each week. (Add this expense to your pregnancy budget.) This should be an amount you can afford to put away. You don't want to find that you can't pay your bills today because you're saving so much. Try to save 10 percent to 15 percent of each paycheck, but make sure it is an amount that you can afford. If you can only afford $50 a month, it is better than nothing. Once you have accumulated some funds (over $500), explore options such as CDs or money market accounts to keep the money in, so that it remains accessible but is also earning a larger interest rate than traditional savings accounts. Continue to save money each week even after your baby is born.

Another way to save is to cut expenses. These might include:

- Using coupons and rebates (save $3 to $5 a week)
- Bringing your own coffee or lunch to work (if you're buying a $3 coffee every morning, you could save $60 a month by bringing your own)
- Using the library instead of buying books or renting videos and DVDs (save $50 a month)

- Eating at home instead of going out (save $200 a month if you eliminate one meal out a week as a couple)
- Turning down the thermostat in your home one degree in winter (save 1 percent of yearly heating costs) and setting the thermostat down five degrees during the day when you are not home (save 10 percent of yearly heating costs)
- Carpooling or using public transportation (save $40 a month)
- Avoiding credit cards unless you pay the balance each month (save 15 percent interest)
- Shopping warehouse stores, sales, and secondhand stores (save $10 a month)
- Canceling your e-mail account and signing up for a free service (save $15 a month)
- Selling items you no longer want on eBay or at a garage sale (earn $20 a week)
- Sending e-cards instead of buying and mailing cards (save $8 a month)
- Withdrawing money from your bank account at the bank, or at an ATM owned by your bank, to avoid ATM fees (if you do a weekly withdrawal, you could save $8 a month)

You can find small savings in many areas of your life. Take the money you would have spent on these things and put it away in a savings account. You will soon find that it adds up quickly.

Your Lifestyle

Childbirth Classes

You will probably want to take a prepared childbirth class when you are in your third trimester. Many insurance plans provide complete or partial coverage for this type of class. Start by contacting your insurer to ask if there are any classes the insurance company sponsors (in which case the cost would likely be low or nothing) or if the insurer can provide you with a list of classes that meet its requirements. While you won't take this class until your seventh or eighth month of pregnancy, it is important to find out now what your coverage is. If you have a co-pay or are not covered, add the cost to your pregnancy budget.

Once you know how many and which classes are paid for, contact the hospital or insurance company who offers them and get a schedule. Most classes are held once a week for four to eight weeks. If you want to take a weekend retreat class, reserve your spot months in advance. Since these are short and intense classes that are completed in one weekend, they are appealing to busy parents and book up quickly.

Here are some popular types of childbirth classes:

- **Lamaze.** The Lamaze method teaches breathing and relaxation techniques and encourages you to rely on a labor partner for support, relaxation assistance, and massage. The goal is natural childbirth, but the methods can be helpful no matter how you give birth.
- **Bradley.** This method stresses the importance of prenatal fitness and nutrition. It relies on deep breathing and looking inward during labor.
- **Hypnobirthing.** These classes use hypnosis to program sleep relaxation into your mind for use during labor.
- **Combination.** These classes teach a variety of methods and options, so that the woman can decide which technique she is most comfortable with.
- **VBAC.** Vaginal Birth After Caesarean classes are designed to help women who have had a previous C-section prepare for a vaginal birth. They focus on strategies for moving labor along and pain and relaxation techniques.
- **Childbirth refresher.** Women who have already given birth once before know the basics but might want some reminders about specific techniques or strategies.

Evaluate classes as follows:

• **Type.** Find out what method the class uses and who sponsors the class. Ask what topics are covered in the class. You want to be sure you learn about the signs of labor, the stages of labor, birth positions, emergency C-sections, coping techniques, medication options, and postpartum care. Some classes will also include basic breastfeeding information and infant care.

• **Schedule.** Is the schedule of the classes compatible with your schedule and your partner's? Find out how long each class is and if breaks are scheduled. Classes longer than two hours each session can seem too long when you're sitting in an uncomfortable chair with a full bladder and big uterus.

• **Location.** Find out where the class will be held and determine if it is convenient to get to. You might also want to ask how many bathrooms there are and how close they are to the classroom. Many a childbirth class has seen a line of ten women anxiously waiting to use the only women's bathroom in the building.

• **Instructor.** Ask about the instructor's qualifications and experience in teaching the course. Many instructors are midwives, labor and delivery nurses, or patient education professionals who have backgrounds in maternity. Labor and delivery nurses and midwives are likely to have had more hands-on experience helping women in labor. Find out if the instructor is a member of the International Childbirth Educators Association (www.icea.org). This is an important certification that shows they meet certain education requirements. Also find out if he or she is certified in any particular childbirth method.

• **Supplies.** Some classes ask you to bring pillows, notebooks, or snacks to share. Find out in advance what you will need to bring along.

• **Cost.** If you will be paying the fee or a portion of the fee yourself, evaluate the cost. You may be able to find lower priced classes if you call around. Remember that you can pay for this class from your FSA if you have one (see Chapter 2 for details).

• **Enrollment.** Classes with large numbers make it hard to ask questions and get personal attention. A class of twelve women or less is a good number.

Once you do schedule a class, make sure you write it on your calendar and on your partner's calendar. If you miss the class, there may not be another one before your due date, so it is important to make attending a priority.

If you don't have time to take a class or there are none near you, consider renting or purchasing a childbirth education videotape or DVD. You can rent DVDs or videotapes from a video store or borrow them for free from your local library.

For more information on childbirth classes, see:

• www.Lamaze.org
• www.BradleyBirth.com
• www.hypnobirthing.com

Childbirth Videotapes/DVDs

Great Expectations: Laugh and Learn About Childbirth (Great Expectations, 2003, DVD $49.95, VHS $54.95).

Transitions to Parenthood (Consumervision, 2002, VHS, $17).

Having Your Baby: A Complete Lamaze Prepared Childbirth Class (Parent Productions, 2004, DVD and VHS, $49.95).

Childbirth from the Inside Out, parts I and II (View, 2003, DVD and VHS, $29.98 each part).

Once you know where and when you'll be taking your childbirth preparation course, find out about other courses sponsored by or reimbursed by your insurer. Other classes include:

• **Breastfeeding basics.** Expectant mothers learn the ins and outs of breastfeeding, including positions, latching on, comfort measures, and nutrition for the breastfeeding mother.

• **Baby care basics.** These classes teach diapering, swaddling, soothing, and bathing techniques, as well as provide information about growth and development and baby proofing.

• **Infant CPR.** Red Cross certified CPR courses teach parents what to do if a baby is choking, stops breathing, or has no pulse.

• **Infant massage.** Learn how to calm, soothe, and bond with your baby using infant massage.

Sibling Classes

If this isn't your first child, you may want to consider taking your older child or children to a sibling class. These classes are offered by hospitals and birth centers and usually focus on children under six. Most instructors recommend enrolling your child around your eighth month of pregnancy, as that is the time when they usually begin to fully see and understand what exactly is happening. The children are introduced to infant care, including diapering and breastfeeding and bottle-feeding, and are taught how to hold a

Books for Kids

Kid's Book to Welcome a New Baby by Barbara J. Collman (Marlor Press, 1999, $12.95).

What to Expect When the New Baby Comes Home by Heidi Murkoff (HarperFestival, 2001, $7.99).

The New Baby at Your House by Joanna Cole (HarperTrophy, 1999, $5.99).

Before You Were Born: A Lift-the-Flap Book by Jennifer Davis (Workman, 1998, $10.95).

baby using lifelike dolls. The instructor will explain to your young child what babies are like, why they cry, why they use diapers, how they eat, and how much they sleep. The children are encouraged to ask questions and play with the dolls. At the conclusion of the class, the children are often taken to see the newborn nursery where they can see real live newborns.

If sibling classes are not available in your area, you can do some education at home with your child. Gradually get him or her used to the idea of being a sibling. Buy a lifelike doll for your child to play with (the Lee Middleton Company, www.leemiddleton.com, sells some) or read books about new babies.

Dental Care

Make plans to see your dentist during your pregnancy. According to the American Academy of Periodontology, pregnancy gingivitis (swelling, bleeding, and redness of the gums) can lead to periodontal disease, which has been linked to low birth weight and preterm labor. If you do develop periodontal disease, a simple treatment (a special type of cleaning) will improve your symptoms and reduce your risk of preterm labor. Obtain regular dental care during pregnancy and report any problems with your gums to your dentist immediately. If your employer offers dental insurance but you have not yet participated, this is a good time to sign up for coverage. Be sure to add your dental expenses to your pregnancy budget.

For more information about periodontal disease and preterm labor, see: www.perio.org/consumer/pregnancy.htm.

83
• • •

Planning Some Mood Lifters

You've probably already experienced mood changes during your pregnancy, and chances are they will continue in the coming months. It can be hard to feel sick, be tired, worry about delivery or parenthood, see your body change, and deal with all the other ordinary stresses of daily life. Start thinking about ways you can lift your spirits and feel good about yourself on those days when you're down in the dumps or in the middle of a crying jag. Try these suggestions:

- Keep a stash of great books or magazines to read.
- Indulge in a favorite treat.
- Ask your partner for a full body massage or treat yourself to one at a spa.
- Go to a movie.
- Learn something new. It's definitely not too late to learn something new like yoga or salsa.
- Get a manicure and/or pedicure.
- Go to the bookstore and look through a pile of pregnancy or baby name books
- Shop for baby outfits.
- Meditate.
- Look at photos of you and your partner as babies and imagine what your baby will look like.
- Call a faraway friend for a good chat.
- Get your hair done (even if you have a friend do it to save money).
- Buy yourself a maternity outfit that is stunning (make sure there is room in your budget).
- Shop for shoes, purses, and jewelry—at least they will still fit after the baby comes (again, check that budget).
- Have a girls' night out with your best friends.
- Do something nice or charitable for someone else.
- Create a scrapbook.
- Plan a weekend getaway (don't forget to consult your budget!).
- Write in your pregnancy journal.
- Make plans for the baby's room.
- Chat online with other expectant mothers.
- Create a family tree so your child has a sense of history.

Getting a Handle on Your Wardrobe

If you haven't already started to shop for maternity clothes, it's probably about time. You may already have had to push some of the tighter items to the side in your closet and focus on the loose or stretchy items. Keep the following tips in mind when buying maternity clothes:

- **Buy items that will mix and match well.** Go ahead and buy patterns and florals but make sure you have some basic solid colors that will go with almost anything.
- **Don't shortchange yourself on weekend clothes or casual wear.** It's tempting to spend all your money on work clothes, but you will want to have comfortable, decent-looking clothes to wear at other times.
- **Don't forget your feet.** Your feet may swell, grow, or experience discomfort. Don't stuff your feet into uncomfortable shoes. If you're a stiletto lady, you may need to add some lower heels to your collection. It's worth the investment to buy one or two pairs of shoes that are comfortable and attractive to get you through your pregnancy.
- **If you will be breastfeeding, start shopping for nursing bras.** Go to a maternity store and get fitted for one so that it will be comfortable and work well. For tips on purchasing bras, see: www.askdrsears.com/html/2/T025200.asp, or www.firstbabymall.com/expecting/parenting/nursingbra.htm.

Once you've started to create a maternity clothes collection, take a hard look at your prepregnancy wardrobe. There are some things that you will be able to continue to wear, at least for a while. But the things that no longer fit might not fit again until months after the baby. Stop torturing yourself and put them away. The good news is that after months of maternity clothes, your prepregnancy wardrobe will feel completely brand new.

Get more tips on maternity clothes online at: www.americanbaby.com/home/maternity-clothes.html.

Books About Maternity Clothes

Hot Mama: How to Have a Babe and Be a Babe by Karen Salmansohn (Chronicle, 2003, $10.95).

Liz Lange's Maternity Style by Liz Lange (Clarkson Potter, 2003, $22.50).

Expecting Style by Lauren Sara (Bulfinch, 2003, $24.95).

Month 4 Checklist

- ☐ Consider possible guardians for your baby.
- ☐ Find out if your state has disability insurance.
- ☐ Find out if your employer has a disability insurance policy.
- ☐ Determine if you are covered under FMLA.
- ☐ Find out if your state has a family and medical leave act.
- ☐ Get dental care.
- ☐ Plan for emergency and unexpected expenses.
- ☐ Select a childbirth class and determine insurance coverage.
- ☐ Consider other types of classes.
- ☐ Plan some fun things for yourself.
- ☐ Get your maternity wardrobe in place.

6

Month 5

J ana and Steve were expecting their first child. They decided
that they wanted Steve's sister and her husband to be
guardians should something happen to them. They decided to
wait until after the baby was born to get their wills made. A few
weeks after the birth of their baby, they were both killed in a car
accident. Because they did not draw up a will indicating their
preference, the court chose Steve's parents. The judge did not
know that Jana and Steve objected to his parents' religious views
and were not comfortable with the idea of them raising their
child.

Your fifth month of pregnancy is exciting because you see your
stomach getting larger, start to feel movement, and know your
baby is growing. The second trimester can be hard, though,
because you are past the initial excitement of finding out you're
pregnant but feel like you still have so far to go until
your baby is born. This is a good time to talk to the
guardian you have selected for your baby and to
consider life insurance.

Your Rights

Understanding Medical Consent Forms

When you enter a birth center or hospital (or when you do preadmission paperwork), you will be asked to sign a consent form. You may also be asked to sign other consent forms as different treatments or procedures (such as an epidural or C-section) become necessary. While medical consent forms are supposed to be understandable by the people who sign them, a study by the *New England Journal of Medicine* found that most are written at a level beyond the average reading level of the general population. Additionally, many people don't take the time to carefully read consent forms since they tend to be long, in small print, and really boring.

Before you sign any form, read it. If you are unable to concentrate (and who can be expected to concentrate on this when in labor?), have your partner read it. Most consent forms say that you agree to be cared for by the facility and to pay for the services. If a form states that you waive liability by the hospital or center, it is usually not a concern, since the hospital or center is always liable for malpractice and negligence. These clauses are boilerplate clauses that mainly make you think the hospital has no liability, but also put the onus of proving fault onto you.

If there is something on a form that you do not understand, ask to have it explained. The hospital or center won't treat you if you don't sign the necessary forms, but you can cross things out and make changes if there is something on the form that you disagree with. For example, some forms state that you agree to be treated by any hospital staff member. In theory this could mean the janitor is allowed to operate. You can cross out this clause and write in that you give permission to your health care provider and any staff that is under his or her direction.

Understanding Fetal Protection Laws

There is a growing movement to hold women responsible for harm caused to their babies during pregnancy. These types of cases deal with drug use, alcohol use, and even a recent case in which a mother was charged for not agreeing to a C-section that could have saved her baby's life. South Carolina has successfully prosecuted women for child abuse for taking drugs while pregnant, and the law also permits prosecution for alcohol abuse. In Iowa, Minnesota, and North Dakota, health care providers must report prenatal drug exposure. In Arizona, Illinois, Massachusetts, Michigan, Utah, Virginia, and Rhode Island, health care providers must test for drug use and report it. The findings can be used for a child abuse case. Wisconsin has a law allowing imprisonment of women who use drugs and alcohol during pregnancy. Not all fetal protection laws are aimed at punishing the mother, though. The federal Fetal Protection Law makes it a separate crime to end the life of a fetus during an attack on the mother, and the Unborn Victims of Violence Act makes it a crime to harm an unborn child during an attack on the pregnant mother.

Talking to Potential Guardians

In Chapter 5 you read about the importance of choosing a guardian for your child. Once you have come up with a potential guardian, or coguardians, it is important to talk to the person or people you have selected to make sure this is a responsibility the guardian(s) would be willing to take on. Most people are honored to be asked to take on such an important responsibility, but others may feel they are too old, too busy, or simply not equipped to deal with it. Because of this, it is important that you talk it over with the person and explain your reasons for making the choice and make sure he or she is comfortable with it. What you would not want is for something to happen to you, have the court be prepared to turn guardianship over to the person you have selected, and have the guardian decide not to accept the responsibility. The court would talk to your other family members and find someone else, but this is a decision that you really want to be able to make yourself. If you select an alternate guardian, it is a good idea to discuss this with the potential alternate as well.

89
. . .

In addition to asking if the person would be willing to take on this responsibility, talk a little bit about your hopes and dreams for your child. Maybe it is important to you that your child go to private school, take dance classes, or go to church. If so, discuss these things with the guardian.

Wills

If you and your spouse do not have wills, your property is divided according to your state's intestacy laws. These are laws that decide how property is divided for people who do not have wills and have not made their wishes known. Usually the property is divided between the surviving spouse and children. Although this may be what you would want, it is still a good idea to be active and make the decision on your own, and a will makes the legal process go more quickly. If your property is distributed under the intestacy laws, the portion that is given to your children would probably be controlled by your spouse (until your children are adults). When you are dealing with a small estate, it often makes more sense for the spouse to be in charge of everything that is left and decide how it can best be used to support the children.

Wills are important also because they allow you to make specific gifts to specific people. Many mothers, for example, feel strongly about leaving certain pieces of jewelry to their daughters. A will can also allow you to leave money or items to specific charities.

In some states it is possible to write your own will, but in general it is best to go see an attorney. In addition to making sure that your will fulfills your state's requirements (such as the right number of witnesses as well as language that clearly meets your state's statutes so there is no confusion about technical things, like who is legally considered to die first if there is a simultaneous death), he or she can help you develop an estate plan that will benefit your growing family.

Once you have your will completed and signed you should talk with your attorney about where best to store it. Some attorneys store wills in safes in their offices. Other attorneys recommend that a will be filed with the county for safekeeping. If you feel strongly about keeping the original will in your home, discuss that option with your attorney. Like any original documents, your will should be stored in a fireproof box, safe, or safe deposit box. The problem with storing the will in your home is that it's possible no one will know it is there. A search is automatically done of the county records when a case comes to probate court. If you file with the county, your will can be found automatically.

Your Finances

Life Insurance

When thinking about their family's future, some parents feel it is important to purchase life insurance for themselves. Some financial experts say life insurance is a good idea, since it guarantees that your spouse or children will be paid a certain amount of money if you die. That money can be used to pay for funeral expenses, as well as to support your family. Other experts feel that it is wiser to take the money you would spend on premiums and invest it in a fairly secure investment vehicle. If you live long enough, you actually will get more for your money, but if you die young, you don't provide that security to your family. However, investment growth is taxable, but life insurance benefits are not.

How Much to Buy

If you decide you want to buy life insurance, it can be hard to know how much to buy. Experts often say that purchasing enough to cover five to ten times your annual income (for each parent) is sufficient. Remember, the amount you are purchasing is the face value of the policy—the amount that is paid out when you die. You will pay a set annual amount that will keep the policy in place. Many employers provide policies as part of a benefits package, so you will want to determine how much coverage you already have. You

LIFE INSURANCE ESTIMATOR

To give you some idea of what kinds of expenses your family will have should you die, complete the following:

　　_____ Your spouse's income, multiplied by eighteen
−　_____ Your family's yearly expenses once your child is born, multiplied by eighteen
−　_____ Funeral costs ($4,000 to $15,000)
−　_____ Cost of college education for your child
　　_____ **TOTAL**

This total is a bare-bones picture of how much additional money your family is going to need to raise your child, without your income, should something happen to you. To calculate the need for your spouse to get insurance, use your income in the first line.

may also have small free policies through your credit union, bank, credit card, or AAA.

Visit www.bygpub.com/finance/LifeInsCalc.htm for a complete worksheet that takes into account life expectancy and prorated future college costs to help you plan how much insurance you need to buy, or talk to your insurance agent.

Types of Life Insurance

There are two basic types of life insurance: term insurance and cash value insurance.

Term insurance is a policy that exists for a set period of time and if you die during that period, the policy pays. Usually the term is one year and is renewable each year. You would pay a premium (fee) each year to keep it in force. If you are under forty, this type of policy is always the least expensive, but it may not be the best value since it does not have a cash value or earn money for you (other policies, see below, function as life insurance but also as investment vehicles that allow you to actually earn money while maintaining coverage). Some term policies are convertible, which means they can be converted to whole life policies at a later date (see below). A convertible policy would be a good choice if you cannot afford a whole life policy right now but want to be able to earn a cash value on your policy in the future when you can afford a better policy.

Cash value life insurance comes in different types—whole life, universal life, and variable versions of these two. They are called cash value because they provide you with insurance (they pay if you die), and they have an amount the policy can be cashed in for. The cash value grows over time. The money you initially invest (to purchase the insurance coverage) earns interest and this interest can be used to pay you a dividend, or you can set up the policy to reinvest the dividend and pay your yearly premium with it. This can be a good plan, since you only make the initial investment in the policy and then it will pay for itself for the rest of your life and you will still have complete life insurance coverage. You can also remove a portion of the cash value of the account balance or you can take a loan against the funds. These can be useful options for a growing family that might need extra money for a home down payment or to pay unexpected medical expenses. Be sure to find out all the available options for any policy you are considering.

Premiums

A premium is the yearly fee you pay to keep your insurance in effect. The amount of your premium will depend on how high a risk the company decides you or your spouse to be. If you have a health condition that may impact your mortality, you would be high risk. The higher your risk, the higher your premium. If you have a dangerous hobby or you are a smoker, your risk will go up. If you have asthma or are overweight, you are considered to be at higher risk and the company wants you to pay more because the odds are they will have to pay your death benefit sooner.

Purchasing During Pregnancy

If you want to buy life insurance, generally it is best to do so before or after pregnancy. While pregnancy is not something that will shorten your life expectancy, it will make underwriters nervous, since you are facing a medical event within a few months. Your partner can purchase at any time.

Comparison Shopping

It is important to shop around when looking for insurance. Different companies do offer different rates. Most states have insurance laws that are meant to make shopping for and comparing policies easier. They require the company to provide you with a net payment index, which will show you the cost of paying for the policy over ten or twenty years. They also must provide you with the surrender cost index (which shows how the policy's value will grow, so that if you plan to take money out, you will know how much will be available). The lower this number is, the less expensive the policy is. If you are considering a policy that invests your money, as with a whole or universal life policy, look at the cash value growth of the policy—how your money will grow over the years—just as you would when considering an investment. In general, it is best if the policy accumulates cash value early on, so that it can continue to reinvest that money and grow. To compare companies, you might also consult *Best's Review: Life and Health*, available at your local library which will show different companies' policy growth.

When considering life insurance, ask these questions:

- What type of insurance policy is this and what is it called?
- How long does the policy last? If it lasts a year, it is a term policy.
- Will the policy earn a cash value?
- Can the cash value be withdrawn, borrowed against, or used to pay the premiums?
- How long will it take to process my application?

- Who will do the medical exam and what is required?
- Will my premiums be at one set amount the rest of my life? Avoid policies with escalating premiums.

Qualifying for and Keeping Insurance

To qualify for insurance you must undergo a medical exam, which is done by a paramedical employed by the insurance company. Once you are approved, your coverage cannot be cancelled unless you fail to pay a premium. You usually have a thirty-day right-of-refusal period once your policy is delivered to you. You can return it within this time frame at no charge.

Life insurance is not like other investments, which you might move around or change depending on the economy. Changing life insurance companies is a bad idea, since every time you do so, you are older and your premiums will be higher. If you have any problems or concerns about life insurance, contact your state insurance department (look in the white government section in your phone book).

Beneficiaries

The beneficiary is the person who receives payment from the policy after you die. The person or people you name must have an insurable interest—meaning they must depend on you financially in some way. Most people select a spouse and/or children. You can also name an alternate beneficiary (so if you name your spouse as beneficiary, you can list your children as alternates). If you already have a policy in place, it is important to change the beneficiary information so that your new child will be a beneficiary, or an alternate beneficiary. Life insurance is not like a will. If you have children born after a will is created, they are treated the same way as children that existed when the will was written. So if you left half your estate to your child, then had another baby, that baby would share the half of the estate you left to your first child. With life insurance, only those people specifically named as beneficiaries can be paid. If you have an existing policy and want to change

95
. . .

it to include your new baby as a beneficiary, you can download the form from your company's website. Print it out now and partially complete it, and send it in after your baby is born (you may need to list his or her birth date and social security number).

Life Insurance for Your Child

Many financial experts believe that it makes more sense to set up investments for your baby instead of purchasing a life insurance policy for him or her. However, some parents want to have the security of knowing that if something happens to their child, funeral expenses will be paid for. If you do purchase life insurance for your child, you will be the policyholder until your child is twenty-one years old. The child then becomes the owner of the policy and can select his or her own beneficiaries.

Your Lifestyle

Naming Your Baby

You probably have looked through baby name books and have started to think about choosing a name for your baby. When choosing a first name, think about a number of things—family heritage, the meaning of names, what sounds right to you, current popular names, and how all of your baby's names will sound together. Middle names are a great way to use family names and first names of relatives you want to honor.

These websites can help you choose a name:

- www.babynames.com
- www.babycenter.com/babyname
- www.ssa.gov/OACT/babynames
- www.babychatter.com
- www.popularbabynames.com
- www.yourbabysname.com

There are plenty of other baby name websites out there. If you are looking for a particular kind of name—for example, you want an Indian name or an Italian name—do a search on: www.google .com and type in "Italian baby names" or "Indian baby names" to find websites devoted to just those types of names. The Social Security Administration compiles lists of the most popular baby names by year. You can see a list of the top ten names from last year, or any year, going back to 1880. You can also type in a name and do a search to find out how popular it has been over the years. Visit www.ssa.gov/OACT/babynames for more information.

Baby Name Books

Beyond Jennifer & Jason, Madison & Montana: What to Name Your Baby Now by Linda Rosenkrantz (St. Martin's Press, 2000, $5.99).

Cool Names for Babies by Pamela Redmond Satran (St. Martin's Press, 2003, $9.95).

75,000+ Baby Names for the 21st Century by Lori Cooper (Lothian Publishing Co., 2000, $15.95).

"A" Is for Adam: Biblical Baby Names by Lorilee Craker (WaterBrook Press, 2000, $7.95).

Complete Dictionary of English and Hebrew First Names by Alfred J. Kolatch (Jonathon David Publishing, 1984, $29.95).

Celtic Names for Children by Loreto Todd (O'Brien Press, 2000, $11.95).

¿Cómo te llamas, Baby?: The Hispanic Baby Name Book by Jamie Martinez Wood (Berkley, 2001, $6.99).

If you are still thinking over names for your baby, it can help to make a list of first and middle names that appeal to you.

BABY NAME WORKSHEET

Use the spaces below to write the names you are considering.

Girl

First Names	Possible Nicknames	Middle Names

Boy

First Names	Possible Nicknames	Middle Names

Try mixing and matching first and middle names in different combinations to see what sounds right. It is also a good idea to select both girls' and boys' names, even if you think you already know what you are having. After you've listed possible names, write any and all nicknames you can think of next to it. While you might love the name Michael, Mikey might not do it for you.

You can choose any last name you would like for your baby. This can include the mother's last name, the father's last name, a hyphenated mix of the two, any other blending of the two, or any other last name you choose, whether or not it has any relationship to you. You make the formal decision about your baby's name when you complete the birth certificate application in the hospital.

Sometimes parents change their minds after they complete the paperwork or after they are home from the hospital. Usually it is not difficult to amend the birth certificate and get it changed, as long as you do so within a month of the birth. Should you need to do this, contact your state department of vital records or vital statistics (do a search on: www.google.com for your state department, or look in the white government guide section of your phone book) and find out what papers you need to complete.

Some parents want to get to know the baby before choosing a name. Bring the application home from the hospital with you and then send the completed form to the hospital or doctor who delivered the baby (find out where to send it before you leave the hospital).

If you and the baby's father are unmarried, you can give your child his last name, even without his permission. But to have him listed as the father on the birth certificate, you must get his consent. Only one state has a law about babies' names. In Florida, if the parents can't agree, the baby receives both parents' last names, hyphenated, in alphabetical order.

When choosing a last name, consider family members' last names and what they mean to you. Some parents feel it is important for everyone in the family to share the same last name. Other parents feel that it is important for a child to carry on a certain last name or to have a last name that represents both parents. There is no wrong choice and you should do what feels most comfortable for you. Some options include:

- Mother's last name
- Father's last name
- Some other family member's last name (for example, grandmother's maiden name)

- A family first or middle name (for example, if many people in your family have Lee as a middle name, use that as a last name)
- Hyphenating mother's last name with father's last name, or vice versa
- Using one parent's last name as a middle name and the other as a last name
- Using one parent's last name as a first name and the other as a last name
- A combination of both parents' last names (for example, taking Williams and Flaherty and creating Willerty)
- Choosing a name that goes with your child's first name or personality

If you take an unconventional approach to choosing a last name, be prepared for the fallout from your families and from people you will encounter in your everyday life. Some families have a hard time understanding why a wife would not take her husband's last name and are even more rigid when it comes to naming children. Many people strongly believe a child must have the same name as his or her father, whether the parents are married are not. Other people are confused if a child does not share a last name with you. (Picture yourself being called Mrs. Long if that's your child's last name.) As your child grows, you may find you have to explain the name. Many people are used to children not having the same name as their mothers, because of divorce or because the parents never married, but they are less understanding when a child does not share a name with either parent. Making the choice is completely up to you, and you should do what feels right and is best for your child.

Month 5 Checklist
- ☐ Discuss guardianship with the person or people you are considering.
- ☐ Talk to your attorney about having a will drawn up.
- ☐ Determine how much life insurance you and your partner currently have or need.

- [ ] If you decide you need more insurance, begin comparison shopping.
- [ ] Locate beneficiary change forms for existing life insurance policies.
- [ ] Consider life insurance for your child.
- [ ] Think about first and last name choices for your baby.

7

Month 6

Karyn planned to give birth at her local hospital. She took her prenatal class there, and when they took the hospital tour, she was struck by how loud and busy it was in the labor ward. The hospital was a teaching hospital, and she was surprised to see interns and medical students moving around the labor ward. Suddenly she knew she wanted to give birth someplace else, but she didn't know what her options were. She did some research online and discovered there were two birth centers in her area, as well as a group of doulas who attended home births. Karyn made up a list of questions and went to talk to the birth centers and doulas. One of the birth centers felt right to her. It was a ten-

Month six is a milestone, since you're two-thirds of the way through your pregnancy. You might feel like you've still got a long way to go, but take a minute to look at how far you've come and how many changes have happened to your body. This is a good month to get a health care directive and to consider the option of banking cord blood. It's also time to start thinking about what your budget will be like once your baby is born.

minute drive from the hospital and an OB was on call at all times. She decided to have her baby there. She was able to do so without complications and went home rested and relaxed.

Your Rights

Health Care Directives

A health care directive is a legal document that lists the kind of medical treatment you consent to, so that should you become unable to make a decision for yourself, your doctors will know your wishes. This is important for treatments that extend a person's life when there is no hope for recovery and when a patient is unconscious and unable to make treatment choices. Although you are having a healthy pregnancy and expect no complications, a health care directive is an important document to have because you don't know when in your lifetime you may need one.

Many people mistakenly assume that their doctors will make the right decisions for them if they are unconscious. But your doctor can't make decisions for you and can only recommend treatment. Doctors are required to extend life, and they can't make the decision to withhold treatment without authorization from the patient or the patient's representative. Health care directives state your preferences for things such as respirators, feeding tubes, resuscitation, and pain medication.

Many people also mistakenly assume that their spouse or family members know the choices they would want and will be able to make the decision for them. In reality, few people talk about what their wishes are and how they would make health care decisions—after all, it's not the happiest of conversation topics. And depending on your state's laws, your doctors cannot just take your family's word for what you might want. It is important that family members have explicit instructions, otherwise the court will not allow the family to make the decision for the patient.

There are several kinds of health care directives. A *living will* specifies what kind of treatment you would choose should you become unable to make decisions for yourself. In some states this document may also include the name of the person you authorize to make decisions for you. A *health care proxy* or *health care power of attorney* names someone else who will make decisions for you if you are unable to and may also explain what wishes he or she would be implementing. If you do not have a health care directive, your next of kin will be asked to make decisions for you about treatment but may not be able to make life-ending decisions if you have not discussed your wishes with him or her.

You can locate your state's health directive form at: http://pub lic.findlaw.com/healthcare/forms.html.

Although your state may have an approved form, it is a good idea to consult with an attorney and have one drawn up that meets your specific wishes, instructions, and feelings. Additionally, some hospitals feel that the state forms can be too vague, so it is a good idea to talk to your attorney and have one created that is specific and includes all of your wishes. If you're going to go to the trouble of completing a health care directive, be sure you do it correctly so it will be valid.

Once you have completed a health care directive, send a copy to your primary care physician and pregnancy care provider. As with all your other documents, keep your health care directive in a safe place since the original may be needed if there is a question. Bring it with you when you go to the hospital. It is not a good idea to give it to the hospital because it may be difficult to get it back when you leave. For health care proxies, be sure to inform your alternate of the location of your form, in the event that the person you named is not available to make decisions for you.

You can change your health care directive at any time. The most effective way is to destroy it and have a new one drawn up. Another choice is to add an addendum to your old document, but you run the risk of the addendum being lost and the old part of the document being used alone.

Cord Blood Preservation

The number of cord blood preservation companies has more than doubled in the past three years, and cord blood banking by new parents is up 50 percent. You have the choice to preserve cord blood, which comes from the baby's umbilical cord. Cord blood contains stem cells that, at the time this book was published, could be used in the treatment of at least forty-five diseases, including leukemia, with new advances occurring daily, according to the American Pregnancy Association.

The cord and the blood contained in it are usually discarded after the birth, but you can choose to preserve some of the blood and the stem cells that are in it. Many people choose to preserve this blood in case the baby ever has an illness that could be treated with the stem cells contained in it.

Cord blood is more compatible than blood harvested from family members and is much simpler to use than harvesting bone marrow from a family member or donor. The American Academy of Pediatrics recommends cord blood banking only if there is a family member with a current or potential need for a stem cell transplant.

Cord blood is harvested from the cord once the cord is cut after birth but before delivery of the placenta. A needle is inserted into the cord (this is painless) and the blood is then placed in a storage container, or the blood is simply allowed to drain out of the end of the cord into a container. The blood is transported to the storage facility and preserved, should it be needed in the future. Many facilities also perform some tests on the blood and provide you with a report.

If you want to bank your baby's blood, you must have arrangements in place before your baby is born. Once the baby is born, the cord will be discarded and it will be too late. You won't be able to make arrangements to preserve it on the spot. If you make the decision to bank the blood, let your health care provider know this. Make sure you obtain the kit from a cord blood bank before your due date so you can take it to the hospital with you.

Costs for cord blood banking vary but often include an up-front enrollment fee and then a payment plan that can be spread out over several years. If you choose to pay the full cost up front, expect to spend close to $2,000. You will be asked to make at least a partial payment when you sign up.

Here are some cord blood banks:

Viacord
866-668-4895
www.viacord.com

Cryo-Cell International
800-786-7735
www.cryo-cell.com

Cord Partners
310-443-4153
www.cordpartners.com

Get a free booklet about cord blood preservation at: www.cor cell.com/AmerPregAssoc108.html?source=AmerPregAssoc108.

Read an online guide to cord blood banking at: www.parents guidecordblood.com.

Contracts

If you choose to go forward with blood cord banking, first choose the right bank for you. You will be asked to sign a contract. When evaluating companies and reviewing contracts, check for the following:

• **Fees.** Make sure all fees are clearly described and you understand when they are due. You want a contract that has a set number of payments. For example, you would not want a contract requiring a payment every month for the rest of your child's life.
• **Services.** Be absolutely clear on the services you are supposed to receive. For example, make sure that transportation and pack-

aging of the cord blood is included in the costs you are given and that lifetime preservation of the blood is part of the contract. Get guarantees as to how the blood will be stored (such as temperature controls).

• **What ifs.** Find out what happens to your baby's cord blood if the facility closes, loses power, or is sold. You want to be sure there is an emergency backup plan in place and that you will have the option of having your baby's blood transferred to a new facility should this one close. Also find out what happens if you miss a payment. You don't want your baby's blood to be discarded without being given notice and an opportunity to make payments or move it elsewhere.

• **Insurance.** Find out if the facility is insured for disasters, malpractice, and errors.

• **Transportation.** Make sure a medical courier is used to transport the blood.

• **Type of storage.** A cord blood bank that only stores cord blood and nothing else opens the storage units less frequently and is more likely to maintain a regular temperature. Find out whether the blood is stored in bags or vials. Vials are less likely to break when frozen.

• **Registration.** Make sure the bank is registered with the Food and Drug Administration. Currently there is no regulation of cord blood banks, but a registration system has been implemented, which is the first step in regulating the industry.

• **Accreditation.** Be sure the bank is fully accredited by the American Association of Blood Banks (check: www.aabb.org).

• **Success rate.** Find out what their collection success rate is and if any blood they have banked has been used successfully in a transplant.

• **Money back.** Find out what happens if your baby's cord blood is for some reason not drawn, lost in transport, or damaged. You should get a refund if any of these situations occur.

• **Use.** Find out how the preserved blood can be withdrawn for use and what information or documentation is needed to do so.

Are there fees for withdrawal and shipping? Can you withdraw a portion or must you withdraw the entire specimen?

Keep information such as your contract and company contact information in a safe place, such as a home safe or safe deposit box. Once your child becomes an adult, pass on the paperwork and contact information for the cord blood preservation to him or her.

Remember to add cord blood banking to your pregnancy budget if you elect to do it.

Donating Cord Blood

You also have the option of choosing to donate your baby's cord blood for research purposes or for use in treating others, such as for treating bone marrow illnesses. Read about donation at: www .marrow.org/HELP/donate_cord_blood.html.

You will need to arrange for cord blood collection as described above, but the cost is paid by the public cord blood bank.

Deciding Where to Give Birth

Where you give birth is an important part of your birth plan (see Chapter 3), but it is important to recognize that it is not one you always will have control over. Depending on when and where you go into labor, you may end up someplace other than you planned. Additionally, some mothers develop health problems that require them to go to a hospital with certain equipment or skilled personnel. You generally have three options: a hospital, a birth center, or at home.

109
• • •

Hospital

You may have a limited number of choices when selecting a hospital because your health care provider may only be affiliated with certain hospitals or because there are only a few hospitals in your area with maternity wards. When choosing a hospital, consider the following:

- Is the hospital a teaching hospital, and are interns or students present during births? If so, you can insist that none be allowed in the room during your baby's birth.
- Are birthing rooms or family-centered care available? These types of rooms are usually more comfortable.
- How well equipped is the hospital to deal with complications? Children's hospitals are better equipped to deal with complications the baby might have.
- Is rooming-in allowed? This is standard in almost all hospitals, but it still pays to ask.
- Is breastfeeding encouraged and are there lactation consultants on staff?
- What is the C-section rate? What is the episiotomy rate?
- Who is allowed to be with you during labor and delivery? Some women want just their labor partner, while others want to invite in the whole family.
- What kind of security is in place? Be sure the hospital always checks armbands and leg bands on babies against the mothers. Ask if fathers wear armbands as well. Ask what procedures they have in place if a security breach happens. There should be a lockdown procedure.
- Is the hospital designated as "baby friendly" by the World Health Organization? (See: www.babyfriendlyUSA.org.) This certification means the hospital encourages breastfeeding and other types of care that are in the best interest of the babies.

Birth Center

A birth center is a choice for many women who want to be in a facility that has some medical equipment but is more comfortable than a hospital. Birth centers are staffed by midwives and often offer birthing options including water birth, birthing balls, birthing chairs, and other alternative choices. Many birth centers are located next to or are attached to a hospital. Birth centers are designed to feel comfortable, with decorated rooms that don't feel institutional. They usually have lower C-section and episiotomy rates than hospitals. Many have kitchens available for use by family members. Birth centers offer more privacy than hospitals and allow you to wear your own clothing. Most women who go to birth centers also obtain prenatal care there, but you can always switch from an OB/GYN to a birth center. They are covered by insurance. Look in the yellow pages of your phone book under Midwives or Birth Centers or do a search on: www.google.com to find one in your area.

A birth center may be for you if:

- You are not having a high-risk pregnancy.
- You have no complicating medical conditions such as diabetes, heart problems, or asthma.
- You do not want an epidural.
- You want to give birth in a relaxed and comfortable setting.
- You want more control over your birth experience.
- You want limited medical intervention.

When evaluating a birth center, visit the facility. Ask the following questions:

- Are the birth attendants licensed in your state?
- What training or certification do they have?
- Who usually attends births?
- How many beds are available and where do you go if there are none?
- Is the center approved by the Commission for the Accreditation of Birth Centers? (See: www.birthcenters.org for more information.)
- Does your insurance policy cover their fees? (Take your card with you when you visit and ask them to determine this.)
- What happens if complications occur? The birth center should have an OB group that provides backup and an agreement with a hospital so they can transfer patients.
- How long has the center been in operation?
- How many deliveries do they do per month?

- What percent of patients are transferred to hospitals?
- What is the C-section rate? What is the episiotomy rate?
- What kind of pain relief is available?
- If a transfer happens, can the midwife go with you?

Home Birth

Some women choose to give birth at home with a doula or midwife present. A midwife has more training and can perform medical tasks, while a doula provides support. Midwives are licensed by the state, but doulas are certified through various organizations, such as Doulas of North America (www.dona.org). A home birth may be for you if:

- You have family and friends who can help care for you after the birth and help run your household.
- You do not have a high-risk pregnancy.
- You want to give birth without any pain medication.
- You have no complicating medical conditions.
- You prefer a birth with as little interference as possible.
- You want your entire family to be present.
- You want to lower your birth costs.
- You want complete control over your birth experience.
- You are worried about exposure to germs in the hospital.
- You live within fifty miles of a hospital.

Home births are different than birth center births because the only equipment available is what the attendant brings with her.

When choosing a doula or midwife for a home birth, consider the following:

- Will she accompany you at home or at the hospital?
- Is she certified? What training does she have? How many births has she handled? How many does she do per month?
- What is included in her fee? Usually a midwife's package includes prenatal and postpartum visits as well as attending the birth.

- What are her backup arrangements if she is unable to attend?
- What is her philosophy of childbirth?
- How does she decide if a patient needs to be transferred to the hospital?
- When during labor will she join you?
- What supplies do you need to obtain?
- How long will she stay after the birth?
- What kind of postpartum care or visits does she provide?

Home birth can be very comfortable, but you must consider emergency care. Determine where the closest hospital is and the fastest way to get there.

For more information about home birth, contact your local midwifery association or visit: www.midwiferytoday.com/articles/home birthchoice.asp.

Hospital Policies

When choosing where to give birth, it is important to understand the facility's set policies. Some examples of hospital policies include:

- Patients must wear gowns.
- Labor coaches cannot be present when you are being prepped for a C-section, when a catheter is inserted, or during the administration of anesthesia.
- Laboring mothers must wear internal or external monitors for the baby's heartbeat.
- Family and friends allowed in the delivery room are limited to a specific number.
- Blood must be drawn once you are admitted for testing.
- No solid food is given to laboring mothers.

113

Every hospital is different, so in order to know what to expect, find out before you are in labor. If you do not take a childbirth class at the hospital, talk to your health care provider about the policies that are in place. Many policies are up to the individual provider, since he or she is the one in charge in the delivery room. If you have any special requests, be sure to ask your health care provider in advance. It's much easier to discuss a policy at your leisure in the doctor's office, than half-naked in the delivery room when you're having contractions.

Some common requests include:

- Being able to eat and drink
- Being able to wear your own clothes
- No internal monitoring and only occasional external monitoring

Your Finances

Planning Your Parenthood Budget

You've planned out how you will manage your finances for your pregnancy and delivery costs, but it's time to start thinking even further ahead. Creating a budget for your new life as parents will help you get a grip on how much money you have coming in and what your set monthly expenses will be. This budget will change as your child grows, of course, but it's very helpful to have an idea, especially in the first few months, of where your money is going. For the first few months, your biggest expenses will be diapers and possibly formula, but as your child grows, you'll be buying baby food, older toys, clothes, and more. Planning a budget is particularly important if one of you will not be returning to work, will be taking some unpaid time off, or will be reducing work hours. Copy this form and fill it out now with the first few months in mind. As your baby grows and your situation changes, revise it with new expenses or changes in your income. Note that this budget is intended to be a complete budget for all of your expenses—those that relate to the baby and those that do not.

You may not have a good idea how much things such as formula or diapers will cost. The next time you are in a grocery or discount store, make note of the prices so you can incorporate an accurate estimate in your budget.

OUR PARENTHOOD BUDGET

Income

Your average monthly joint take-home income for
   the first three months   _____
Other sources of income, such as dividends, interest,
   eBay sales, etc.   _____

Total Monthly Income   _____

Expenses

Home

Mortgage/rent   _____
Electricity   _____
Gas   _____
Cable or satellite TV   _____
Telephone and cell phone   _____
Internet   _____
Water   _____
Property taxes (if not included in your mortgage
   payment; yearly costs divided by twelve)   _____
Homeowner's or renter's insurance (yearly costs
   divided by twelve)   _____
Condo association fees (yearly costs divided
   by twelve)   _____
Home equity loan payments   _____
Home maintenance   _____
Household supplies   _____

Lawn/yard maintenance _____
Household supplies for cleaning and upkeep _____
Household furnishings (purchases and maintenance) _____
Other household purchases _____

Transportation

Car payments or bus/subway fare _____
Car maintenance and repairs (yearly costs divided
   by twelve) _____
Driver's license, registration, inspection (yearly costs
   divided by twelve) _____
Insurance (yearly costs divided by twelve) _____
Gas _____
Car washes _____
Tolls/parking _____

Personal Expenses

Grocery shopping for you and your spouse _____
Grocery items for baby (diapers, formula, wipes,
   cereal, baby food, etc.) _____
Eating out/takeout _____
Clothing for you and your spouse _____
Clothing, bedding, linens for baby (including
   christening gown or other special items) _____
Breastfeeding supplies _____
Bottle-feeding and feeding supplies _____
Laundry/dry cleaning/tailor _____
Additional laundry expenses for baby _____
Haircuts and styling _____
Internet and e-mail _____
Postage _____
Personal care (nails, salon, etc.) _____
Gym membership _____
Classes (infant CPR, Mommy and Me, etc.) or
   other activities with baby _____
Health insurance _____

Prescriptions   _____

Medical co-pays and deductibles (including
   well-baby visits)   _____

Cord blood bank payments   _____

Charitable donations   _____

Household help   _____

Income taxes   _____

Pet expenses   _____

New baby equipment and supplies   _____

Day care or nanny   _____

Educational books, DVDs, or videos   _____

Other: _____   _____

_____   _____

_____   _____

Entertainment

Toys for baby   _____

Newspapers, magazines, books, and music   _____

Books for baby   _____

Music for baby   _____

Movies, DVD rentals, theater, concerts, etc.   _____

Babysitting   _____

Gifts   _____

Party supplies   _____

Wrapping paper, supplies, and cards   _____

Vacation (yearly costs divided by twelve)   _____

Birth announcements, christening invitations, and
   thank-you notes   _____

Financial

Credit card interest and payments   _____

Bank fees   _____

Life insurance payments   _____

Automatic savings   _____

Payments to 529 plan or other college fund
   for baby   _____

117
• • •

Student loan payments _____

Retirement plan payments _____

Other loan payments _____

Investments or bank accounts for child _____

Legal fees (for will, health care directives, etc.) _____

Other: _____ _____

_____ _____

_____ _____

Total Monthly Expenses _____

This worksheet helps you see what you can expect to spend per month once you are a parent. If your monthly expenses are higher than your monthly income, take a good hard look at your expenses and see what you can eliminate or reduce.

Your Lifestyle

Registering for Shower Gifts

It is helpful to register for gifts before a shower so that people have a sense of what you need and want. Some moms hate the idea of registries, but if you'll be getting gifts from people who hardly know you, it is a sensible way to provide ideas for gifts. Even if you are not planning a shower, a baby registry can be a good idea. It's likely that people will want to visit you and bring gifts after the baby is born, and a registry is simpler than trying to tell each person exactly what you need.

Decide where you want to register. Some mothers register at more than one place. This can be smart if none of your local stores have a big selection. Choosing a national chain can be a good idea, since most post the registries online and friends and family who are not in your local area can then shop online for you. It is also convenient for those who do live close to you so that they can view your list before heading into the store. In addition, it's easier for you because you can create your registry from the comfort of your home. Some chains with online registries include:

- www.Target.com
- www.USABaby.com
- www.BabiesRUs.com

If you do not have a national chain in your area, you can still create an online registry if your local baby store belongs to: www.MyBabyRegistry.com.

Completing Your Registry

What could be more fun than shopping without having to spend any money? When choosing items for your registry, look at your pregnancy budget and make note of items you have not purchased. Register for items from your budget but also register for items you had not thought of before that you see in the store or on the website. There are probably items you would like to purchase on your own; for example, some parents like to know that they personally paid for a crib and, if that is the case, don't register for those things.

Next, think about the items you really need. There are a lot of must-have items and there are two ways to think about them. Some parents list these on their registries and then plan to go out and purchase things they did not receive after the shower so that they are fully equipped once the baby comes. Other parents feel that they would rather be in control of the must-have items and instead use the registry to ask for items they would like but don't absolutely need immediately. It's important to remember that a lot of gift givers shop without using registries, or look at the list and then purchase items elsewhere, so if you go out and buy all of the basics, you may find that people give you items you've already bought.

There are a few basic categories of items to register for:

- **Clothing.** It can be hard to know what size your baby is going to wear and when, so stick to registering for newborn and size

3 months. Make sure you register for different types of clothing—Onesies, sleepers, socks, sweaters, hats, and sleep sacks.

- **Linens, blankets, towels, and bibs.** One hundred percent cotton sheets tend to shrink unless you choose high-quality items. You will probably receive many blankets and bibs, so only register for a few.
- **Toys and soothing items.** You may not know what brand of pacifier your baby prefers until you actually try them, so don't register for too many of one brand.
- **Feeding.** If you're planning to breastfeed, be sure to register for a few bottles so you can pump. Don't forget about comfort items for nursing.
- **Diaper and bath items.** These include a tub, washcloths, diaper disposal system, etc.
- **Equipment.** This includes a car seat, swing, changing pad or table, monitor, crib, and high chair.

Remember that you might need two of some items—a breast pump at home and at work, an additional car seat for your mom who will be babysitting, or extra crib sheets to use at day care.

It's tempting to register for or buy items that are cute or pretty, but think about what your needs will be and how the product fits them. A good place to start is the Juvenile Products Manufacturers Association at: www.JPMA.org, where you can get tips about safety and selection. Talk to your friends and relatives who have babies and get some opinions about various products. A car seat may look wonderful, but if it is hard to install or difficult to buckle, you will soon think it's not so wonderful at all. Additionally, you may wish to consider models that will give you extended use, such as a convertible car seat or a crib that converts to a headboard. You can get some parents' opinions on websites such as: www.epinions.com, or www.bestbabyproducts.com.

If you go into a store to register, you may wish to ask a sales associate to assist you. Some stores ask that you make an appointment if you want to have someone help you. Other stores send you off on your own with a list to write on or a handheld scanner you can use to scan the UPC codes of the items you want to buy. It can start to feel like a big shopping spree, and it's easy to get out of control with it quickly, so come into the store with a list of the types of items you want to register for. Feel free to add items you see that you hadn't thought of, but try not to go overboard.

Get a copy of the list because many stores offer you a discount if you come in to purchase items you registered for but did not receive. This is a good reason to register for absolutely everything you will need to buy or to register even if you won't have a shower. People will still buy you new baby gifts and you can come in and buy everything else you need at a discount. Be sure to ask about the store's discount policy when you register.

If you are going to have more than one shower, or expect that people will use the registry to purchase gifts once the baby arrives, update the list once you've received gifts. Some gift givers forget to notify the registry when they've made a purchase and/or buy items that are similar to those on the registry.

Books About Shopping for Baby Items

Baby Bargains: Secrets to Saving 20% to 50% by Alan Fields (Windsor Peak Press, 2003, $16.95).

Consumer Reports' Best Baby Products (Consumer Reports, 2004, $16.95).

Organizing Warranties and Instructions

As you start to buy and receive baby items, save the warranties so if an item breaks, you will be able to contact the manufacturer to get it repaired or replaced. Send in any warranty registration forms (or register online). Start collecting your warranty information into an accordion folder (filed alphabetically) or in a plastic storage box. Write the date the item was purchased or received on the form itself so that you will have a firm date for when the warranty expires.

121
• • •

Save instruction manuals or assembly information with warranties. You might move and need to take the crib apart and reassemble it, and that can be hard to do without the instructions. Instructions also list model numbers and manufacturer contact information should you ever need a replacement part.

Beginning to Plan Your Nursery

You might have a room in mind for your baby's nursery (or you might have part of a room in mind), but now it is time to begin thinking seriously about how you will organize the room. Before you buy furniture and accessories, consider the bare bones of the room:

• **Flooring.** Is the room carpeted? Wall-to-wall carpet reduces noise and provides a comfortable place for the baby to play. If you are purchasing carpet, be sure to open the windows during installation, since the carpet is treated with chemicals. Clean the floor underneath before installation. If your baby's room has wood or laminate flooring, check its condition to see if it is warped, lifting up, or peeling. If so, arrange for replacement or repair. If a hardwood floor will be refinished, be sure you leave the house or ventilate during the work.

• **Walls.** Decide if you will paint or wallpaper the walls. Painted walls are most versatile, since you can easily change the color or put up a border or decals to change the look. If you will be painting, consult your health care provider for information on what type of paint you should avoid (fumes can be dangerous to pregnant women).

• **Lighting.** If you have an overhead light in the room, consider installing a dimmer switch so the light won't be blinding in the middle of the night, or plan on buying a tabletop lamp.

• **Heating and cooling.** A ceiling fan is an easy way to cool the room in the summer and is much safer than a box fan or tabletop fan. Check the windows to be sure they lock and close completely. Remove miniblinds, since they pose a strangulation danger. Make sure the heating vents or radiators in the room work well, and make note of the location of those as well as air-conditioning vents when you began to plan your room layout (see Chapter 8).

Checking Your Home for Lead and Other Hazards

If your home or apartment was built before 1978, it may contain lead paint. Lead paint is a neurotoxin and, when ingested, can impact a child's mental growth and development. When lead paint flakes, disintegrates, or peels, particles are released into your home. If your baby mouths a toy that has lead dust on it, he or she can ingest it. Toddlers also might eat flakes of lead paint they find on floors or windowsills.

If you suspect lead paint is in a home you own, contact the National Lead Information Hotline (800-532-3394, or www.epa .gov/lead/nlic.htm) for the name of a company in your area that can do lead testing. In many states, if lead paint is found and you wish to remove it or have it encapsulated, you must hire a certified contractor.

If you rent your home or apartment, contact your landlord and ask for information about lead paint on the premises. If you believe there may be lead paint in your rental unit and your landlord is not cooperating, send him or her a written letter indicating that you believe there is deteriorating lead paint on the premises and request that it be repaired. If you get no response, contact the National Lead Information Hotline. Your landlord is required to provide you with a rental unit that is fit to live in. The presence of disintegrating lead paint makes it unfit, and he or she is required to fix it. Doing so can be expensive, and your landlord might not understand the risk, so you may need to talk to local housing authorities and to someone at the National Lead Information Hotline to get some assistance.

For more information about lead paint, see:

- www.cdc.gov/nceh/lead/faq/about.htm
- www.epa.gov/lead

- www.leadlisting.com
- www.afhh.org

You may also wish test your home for radon. Learn more at www.epa.gov/radon.

Buying Baby Care Books

Sitting down and reading an entire baby care book from cover to cover might be more than you can contemplate right now, so try to read a few pages a day or read only the newborn sections, saving the rest to read once the baby is born (and hoping that you can find the time then!).

Baby Care Books

The Mother of All Baby Books by Ann Douglas (John Wiley and Sons, 2002, $15.99).

The Baby Book by James Sears (Little, Brown and Company, 2003, $21.95).

Caring for Your Baby and Young Child by the American Academy of Pediatrics (Bantam, 1998, $20.00).

Buying a Breast Pump

If you plan on breastfeeding, think about purchasing a breast pump (or adding it to your shower registry). Even if you plan to feed on demand and take your baby with you everywhere, you will eventually need a break, and a breast pump will give you some freedom. You have the option of renting a hospital-grade pump, which pumps more efficiently and more quickly and may be useful if you have twins or a premature birth or if you will be working. Check into rental costs if this is something you are interested in. Look in your phone book under breastfeeding supplies, or call a medical supply store.

When choosing a breast pump, consider whether you want manual, battery-powered, electric, or convertible (both electric and battery-powered). Battery-powered and convertible pumps allow you to use them anywhere, but electric and convertible pumps tend to have more powerful suction.

Look for pumps that allow you to pump both breasts at the same time, something that will be a great time-saver. Make sure the suction level can be adjusted to your comfort level. Check the cycling time. The faster the cycling time, the more times it will apply suction per minute and the faster your pumping will go.

For more information about choosing a breast pump, go to:

- http://breastfeed.com/resources/articles/breastpump.htm
- www.askdrsears.com/html/2/T023500.asp

Month 6 Checklist

☐ Have a health care directive prepared, or update an older one, and notify your health care provider.

☐ Consider banking or donating cord blood.

☐ Sign up for a cord blood program if you decide to bank the blood.

☐ Let your care health care provider know if you will be banking cord blood.

☐ Decide where you would like to deliver your baby.

☐ Determine what the policies are at your hospital or birth center.

☐ Create a parenthood budget.

☐ Register for shower gifts.

☐ Devise a system for organizing warranties and instructions.

☐ Plan the bare bones of your nursery.

☐ Consider home hazards you may wish to test for.

☐ Buy and begin to read baby care books.

☐ Buy or register for a breast pump if you will be breastfeeding.

8

Month 7

Leah and her husband were expecting twins. She planned to take nine months off from her job as a legal secretary and then return to work, leaving the babies with a sitter. When she and her husband crunched the numbers and included the employer withholding they would have to endure, it soon became clear that hiring a full-time sitter was too expensive. A friend of Leah's recommended an au pair, and Leah and her husband found this to be the perfect solution for them. The agency dealt with all the paperwork, Leah and her husband were able to pay a reasonable amount for child care, and they were able to obtain full-time live-in care for their babies.

You made it to the third trimester! It may feel like things are really speeding up now, with your baby's birth only a few months away. It's time to firm up plans for time off after the baby, choose a pediatrician, and make decisions regarding day care or nannies.

Your Rights

Choosing a Pediatrician

You're going to spend a lot of hours in the pediatrician's office in the coming years, so it is important that you choose one you are comfortable with and whom you can trust. One of your primary concerns should be location. Since you are going to go there often, find an office that is convenient to get to and relatively nearby. You don't want to have to drive for an hour with a feverish, sobbing child in the back seat.

Another important factor to consider is how comfortable you are with the doctor and the practice. Although you will be selecting one doctor to be your child's primary health care provider, you're going to see a lot of the other doctors and personnel in the office, so you must be sure you're comfortable with the entire practice. It makes the most sense to choose a pediatrician who accepts your health insurance. However, if you feel strongly about a pediatrician who does not participate in your plan, explore what the out-of-network costs are and whether you are willing to pay them.

If you don't know whom to choose for a pediatrician, ask your family and friends for recommendations. Your own doctor can also recommend pediatricians in your area. If there is an office near your home, you may wish to consider it as well. To find pediatricians in your area, you can use the American Academy of Pediatrics' online referral service at: www.aap.org/referral.

Make an appointment with your top choices for a consultation. Most consultations are free, but some doctors do charge for the time, so ask when you make the appointment.

In the waiting room look for:

• **Separate sick and well waiting rooms.** These should be entirely separate rooms with separate reception desks. If there is only one room, well children are exposed to sick children. Most pediatricians now adhere to this standard, but some simply do not have the room.

• **The number of people waiting.** If the room is packed, there's a chance the office does not schedule appointments well. Ask the nurse or receptionist how many appointments the doctor takes in a day and how long the typical wait time is. Ask if today's wait is typical.

• **Toys, books, videos.** See if there are enough toys and books for the children who are waiting and if they are clean and in good condition. Some offices play videos, which can be a lifesaver if you're waiting for a long time.

• **The overall feel of the room.** Does it feel comfortable, pleasant, and safe? Is there enough seating for everyone? Are tissues available? Is there a place to hang coats?

When you meet with the doctor, notice the following:

• **The staff.** An aide or nurse will probably take you to a conference room or an exam room. Notice if he or she is pleasant and friendly. Also note whether the staff at the front desk is friendly. As you move through the hallways, look to see how the staff is interacting with the children and parents in the office.

• **The doctor's demeanor.** Is he or she friendly and relaxed or rushed and short with you? Think also as to whether this is someone you think a small child could feel comfortable around.

Ask the doctor the following questions:

• **Which hospitals do you practice at?** If your area has a children's hospital, you will probably want a doctor that has privileges there. Make sure the doctor has privileges at the hospital you plan to deliver at.

• **What are your hours?** Are there evening or weekend hours? More practices are scheduling these types of hours to accommodate working parents.

• **How are calls handled after hours?** You want a practice that has an answering service and a doctor on call at all times. Some practices have a service and then a nurse. If this is the case, make sure a doctor is on call and can be reached.

• **How long have you been in practice?** Where are his/her degrees from?

• **Who is on staff?** Ask the names of the other doctors and other professional staff, such as lactation consultants, nurse practitioners, and physician assistants. Find out who handles what. Think about whether you want to be at a large practice with many doctors or a smaller one.

• **How long is a typical wait?** You probably don't want to have to wait more than half an hour. Also, be aware that most offices will tell you the amount of time spent in the waiting room and fail to add in the time spent in the exam room waiting for someone to come in.

• **Do you have a newsletter or e-newsletter through which you regularly communicate with parents?** This can be useful because it will let you know about changes in hours, staff changes, and important health information, such as when flu shots will be available.

• **What is your position on antibiotic usage?** The American Academy of Pediatrics recently changed its policy about the use of antibiotics for ear and sinus infections, recommending that pediatricians take a wait-and-see approach and avoid prescribing antibiotics when possible, to help prevent the problems with antibiotic resistance.

• **What are the phone hours?** Are doctors and nurses available to take questions at specific times? Are there special hours when parents can call in and speak directly to the doctor? Will they communicate by e-mail?

• **What is your phone system like?** Can it handle the volume of calls they get? Are there voice-mail boxes and policies about how quickly calls will be returned?

• **Who pinch-hits?** If the doctor is not part of a large practice and works on his or her own, who handles this when he or she is off duty?

- **How far in advance are well appointments made and how easy is it to change appointment times?** Do they have a cancellation policy?
- **Do you participate in my health insurance plan?** Since you will have to pay extra for an out-of-network physician, it is usually best to choose someone who accepts your insurance.
- **What do I need to do to have you become my child's health care provider?** You may need to notify your health insurance company in advance, but usually you just notify the hospital when you check in and they will contact your doctor.

Locating Child Care

If you plan to return to work or school once you've completed your leave time, think about day care options now, so that you can get your child enrolled or have a place held for him or her with the caregiver you select.

Day Care by Family Members

When you decide to have a relative care for your baby, you must first decide where the care will take place—at your home or theirs. Initially, at least, it can be easier to have the baby cared for at your home. Have a frank talk about pay. Find out if the relative expects to be paid and, if so, negotiate something fair. If he or she does not want compensation, set an allowance for expenses, such as gas and other items that he or she may have to pay out of pocket.

Be very clear about your child-raising techniques. Some grandparents can be resistant to "new" ideas such as putting a baby to sleep on her back, time-out, breastfeeding, or feeding on demand. Make sure that your decisions and choices as a parent will be respected. If the relative will be caring for your baby at his or her own home, talk about child safety and the kinds of modifications that might be necessary once the baby is mobile, such as blocking off stairs and covering outlets. If he or she will be driving with the baby, make sure a car seat will be properly used and installed in

131

the vehicle. Make sure that any baby equipment at the home is up to modern standards. Many grandparents want to reuse cribs and high chairs they saved from their own children, but these usually do not meet modern safety standards (for more information on standards, contact the Juvenile Products Manufacturer's Association at: www.jpma.org).

Make sure the drop-off and pick-up schedule is conducive for both of you. Arrange whether you will transport the baby to and from the relative's home. Consider how much time this will add to your commute and whether this will increase your expenses (due to tolls or more mileage) and add this to your parenthood budget.

Day Care Centers

When choosing a day care, it is essential that you not only interview the director, but also that you spend time at the facility (at least two visits). Read your state's day care licensing requirements at: www.americatakingaction.com/childcare/licensing.html, or at the National Child Care Information Center at: http://nccic.org so that you know what the requirements are. Call your state licensing agency and find out if any complaints have been made about the center and if any investigations are pending. When you visit facilities, find out what the policies are concerning:

- **Sleeping.** Are infants allowed to follow their own schedules or are they required to nap at certain times? Does each baby have a separate crib? Do parents provide bed linens? It is best if each child has a separate crib and if babies are permitted to follow their own schedules. Make sure children are supervised even when they are sleeping.
- **Schedules.** Does the center accept full-time and part-time children? What are their normal hours of operation? What holidays are they closed on? What is their policy for closings due to weather or emergencies? Is there a minimum number of days you must send your child for?
- **Safety.** Do cribs, toys, and equipment meet safety standards and are they checked regularly for safety? Are there any floor-

length windows or glass doors that could pose a threat to children? These need to be blocked off. If there are miniblinds, are the cords out of reach? Are bookcases attached to the walls? Are electrical outlets covered? Are lighting fixtures out of reach? Are outdoor play areas fenced? If the children take walks, how is safety managed? Are fire drills practiced? Is there an emergency plan in place in the event of a disaster or a terrorist attack? Does the center meet local fire codes? Are there smoke alarms in each room? Are there enough emergency exits? Make sure the facility meets your standards for safety and that policies are in place that protect your child.

• **Cleanliness.** How often are toys, cribs, high chairs, swings, floors, linens, tables, and rocking chairs sanitized? What are they sanitized with? It is best if all equipment is sanitized after each use and toys after they are mouthed. Are cloth diapers allowed or are only disposables used? Find out where diapers are changed, what the policy is about hand washing after diaper changes (staff hands should be washed every single time and the diaper-changing area sanitized each time), and how diapers and wipes are disposed of. All diapers and wipes should be removed from the room if possible.

• **Feeding.** Are mothers encouraged to come in to breastfeed if they wish? Do parents provide formula or expressed milk as well as bottles? It is best if parents supply milk or formula in their own bottles and if the center encourages and supports nursing mothers. Find out if infants are fed on demand or on a schedule. A schedule may make it easier for the center, but your child might have a hard time adjusting to a schedule. Do parents provide baby food and feeding utensils? Cleanliness is more certain if you send these items. Are these items labeled to prevent mix-ups? Are all food and beverage items refrigerated?

• **Staff.** What is the average age and education level? How are staff members chosen and what references or background checks are required? A degree in early childhood education is best. The staff should be trained in infant CPR, have current immunizations, and get the flu shot each year. Make sure the staff is screened for criminal backgrounds as well as child abuse. Make sure that no one other than a trained staff member will be caring for your child. Find out if there is a director or head staff person present at all times. The minimum acceptable child-to-staff ratio is one staff member to four infants. Does the center use interns or student teachers and, if so, how are they screened? Make sure a paid staff member is always observing these types of staff members.

• **Rooms.** Are there different rooms for infants, toddlers, and preschoolers? It is usually best if the age groups are kept separate because they have different needs and schedules. Ask if rooms are rotated, so that children are not in the same room all day.

• **Outdoor activities.** Is there a fenced outdoor area or regular walks? How are children supervised outdoors? Is the playground equipment safe (with recycled tires or other cushioning material underneath it), arsenic free, and properly supervised? Is sunscreen and/or bug repellant applied before outdoor play?

• **Health.** What are the vaccine requirements for children and staff? They should be the same as the recommendations of the American Academy of Pediatrics (online at: www.cispimmunize .org/IZSchedule.pdf). What symptoms require you to keep your child home? Most centers say that if your child has a fever or is vomiting, you should keep him or her home. The policy should limit exposure but be broad enough so that you can actually get to work most days. Is there a nurse or physician retained by the center to deal with medical emergencies? There should be one associated with the center on call.

• **Absences and vacations.** Are you responsible for paying for days that your child does not attend? Most centers require this, since they have to pay staff to be there. Can you take vacations and not have to pay for the time you are away? Some centers provide sick or vacation days you can use throughout the year without additional fees and may allow you to purchase more at a rate lower than what you would pay if your child attended that day.

• **Parent involvement.** Some centers encourage or require parents to visit, spend time at, or help out at the facility. Make sure at the very least that parents are permitted to stop in and visit anytime they wish to. Ask if the center has an online camera showing a live feed from the center. This way you can check up on your child anytime.

- **References.** Ask for references and ask to speak with parents of children enrolled there.
- **Fees.** Do you pay a daily rate or an hourly rate? Is there a yearly registration fee? If your child will be there for extended periods, an hourly rate may cost you more. Can you schedule your child for additional time if necessary? Are there additional fees if you are late picking up your child? Is there a yearly registration fee? What other fees exist? For example, some centers charge for diapers if you forget to bring them. Some centers ask parents to provide snacks or fruit on a rotating basis or have monthly baby-wipes charges. Find out everything you are expected to pay for or provide and add this to your parenthood budget.
- **Items from home.** Can you bring items from home such as toys, blankets, pacifiers, and extra clothes? How must these items be labeled and when are they sent home for washing?
- **Bathrooms.** Make sure children are not isolated or alone when they use the bathroom. An isolated bathroom makes child abuse much easier. A bathroom should be easily accessible from the room where the child care is taking place. Look for centers with child-size toilets and ask how the center ensures that children have privacy while toileting.
- **Discipline.** What behavior modification methods are used? Time-outs are most common for toddlers and preschoolers and no physical punishment should be allowed. Are the discipline methods consistent with all staff members?
- **Liability issues.** Does the center have a contract that removes them from all liability? Be suspicious if this is the case. Are they insured? Make sure they are.
- **Climate.** Are the rooms adequately heated and cooled? Are the rooms vented to allow fresh air to circulate? Are the rooms bright and filled with natural light? Look for a center that looks, smells, and feels comfortable, clean, and welcoming.

Read your contract carefully. You may be asked to sign a consent form allowing emergency medical care to be obtained for your child in your absence. It may also be useful to sign consent forms that will allow other people (such as a grandparent) to pick your child up should you be unavailable. If the center does not have a consent form, make your own:

Day Care Consent Form

I, _____ , parent of _____ ,
          your name   child's name

who is in your care at _____ , hereby
                                    name of center

authorize _____ to pick my child up at
                    authorized person's name

any time without any further permission needed from me.

_____   _____
                signature   date

Payments to a day care center can be applied toward the child care credit on your tax return. The credit entitles you to deduct 20 percent of your income, up to $2,400 (see IRS publication #503 at: www.irs.gov).

In-Home Day Care Centers

In-home day care centers are run in someone's home and typically have only one or two caregivers. Usually, a small number of children are cared for. In-home care centers can feel less institutional and the schedule may be more flexible. However, the caregiver has less backup and is likely to have fewer resources available in terms of toys, games, and equipment.

Even though this type of day care is run in someone's home, there are state regulations and licensing requirements. To find your state's regulations, visit: www.daycare.com/states.html. Make sure any in-home day care you consider is licensed by the state. Call the state licensing agency and find out if any complaints have been made or if any investigations are pending.

When considering in-home day care, ask the same questions as those listed above for day care centers, as well as about the following:

- **Safety.** How are children kept separate from the rest of the home? Are children permitted in the kitchen and, if so, what safety precautions are in place? It is preferable if there is one area of the home set aside for child care and the kitchen is not accessible by the children.
- **Paying clients' children versus caregiver's own children.** Will the caregiver be caring for her own children as well as those of paying clients? If this is the case, you may want some assurance that her children will not take precedence.
- **Staff.** Are there any other caregivers? What is their training and background? Who cares for the children if the owner is ill?
- **Pool.** Is there a pool? If so, it should be completely fenced and inaccessible. Wading pools should be used with supervision and emptied when not in use.
- **Transportation.** Are the children transported anywhere by the day care caregiver? If so, in what kind of vehicle? Are car seats provided? Make sure you know where your child is going to be and when. Be certain the caregiver is insured and that all children in the vehicle are in car seats.

Nannies and Sitters

There are a variety of in-home child care options to consider.

Agency Nannies When choosing a nanny or a sitter you may wish to use an agency. Agencies prescreen candidates and many handle payments, so you do not need to do payroll taxes. To locate an agency, ask friends and family for recommendations or look in your yellow pages under Nanny or Child Care. Make an appointment with the agency to discuss your needs and the types of caregivers they have available. You may be asked to register with the agency and complete a form that indicates the length and type of care you are looking for.

If you are hiring a nanny through an agency:

- Make sure you have final selection of the nanny you will hire.
- Confirm that employment taxes and withholding will be done by the agency.
- Find out how quickly a replacement is available if your nanny leaves or you fire her.
- Determine the type of screening process that is used to select their nannies.
- Ask if nannies are all U.S. citizens and, if not, whether they have visas and how long they are going to be in the United States.
- Ask if the agency does spot checks. This is an extra protection for you.
- Make sure nannies come with references and check them yourself, or at least ask to see them.
- Determine the minimum training and education that is required. Nannies with degrees in early childhood education are usually preferred.
- Find out if there are basic agency rules the nannies must comply with—for instance, rules that the nannies do not do housework, other than cleaning up after the children.
- Try to use an agency that has come recommended to you by someone else.
- Ask what the hourly or day rate is.

Au Pairs You might also consider an au pair. An au pair is usually a foreign citizen here on a visa. These young women live with you full-time and provide child care in exchange for a place to live, transportation, meals, and a stipend. Au pairs usually have little or no experience in child care and are really more like exchange students who are here to gain cultural experience. Au pairs are placed through au pair agencies (look under Nanny or Child Care in your yellow pages). When interviewing an au pair service ask about:

- **Selection.** How are the girls chosen? Does the agency seek them out or do they apply? Find out what qualifications, minimum age, and education are required. Many au pairs are young and may not have completed college.
- **Cost and housing.** What is the cost and what are the housing requirements? Au pairs must have their own bedrooms.
- **Language.** How well do the girls speak English? Make sure they have taken English classes.
- **Length of placement.** How long is the placement normally for? Usual time is one year.
- **Replacements.** How long does it take to get a replacement if the au pair decides to go home or you decide she is not working out?

Independent Nannies or Sitters If you hire a nanny or a sitter yourself, call the references and ask detailed questions such as:

- How long did she work for you?
- When did she work for you?
- How old were the children being cared for?
- Why did she leave?
- Would you hire her again?
- Did your children like her?
- Did you have any problems or complaints?
- Do you recommend that I hire her?
- What did you like best about her?
- Was she reliable, on time, and friendly?

Conduct a careful personal interview. Be very clear about what the responsibilities, hours, and pay will be. Discuss the following:

- Get details about her experience caring for infants and about any education or training she has in child care.
- Determine if she has transportation or a driver's license.
- If she is not from this country, how long does she plan to stay and how long is her visa for?
- Confirm when she is available to start, the hours she is available, and the pay.
- Find out what kinds of activities she plans to do with your baby.
- Determine if she will take your child outside and, if so, what the boundaries are that you want her to respect.
- Find out if she is available for evenings or weekends as well as daytime hours.
- Discuss whether you will provide her meals or if she will bring them.
- Discuss home safety and cleanliness rules you want her to follow.
- Find out her feelings about methods of getting a baby to sleep.
- Get her thoughts about schedules and feeding on demand.
- Find out if she cooks and, if so, what kinds of things she will prepare.
- Discuss her views on behavior modification.
- Ask if she is trained in CPR.
- Ask if she has a cell phone for emergencies.
- If she is not going to be working for you full-time, will she be working for other families as well?
- Listen to her speech and determine if you think she has an accent or is easy to understand.

You can do some further checks on your own. Check your state's sex offender registry to make sure the nanny or sitter is not registered. Access your state's registry online at: www.prevent-abuse

-now.com/register.htm. To do an in-depth background check, you can pay a private investigator or a background check company to do a brief criminal record check. You can also request that any person applying for the job go to the local police department and request a criminal records search and obtain a certificate stating they have no criminal background (this is routinely required for people who are adopting, so it is not out of the ordinary). If you want to do a background check on your own, visit www.casanet .org/program-management/volunteer-manage/criminal-bkg-check .htm to learn what kind of access to criminal convictions your state permits.

Live-In Nannies If you are hiring a live-in nanny, make sure:

- Her hours are clearly designated. She will not be on call twenty-four hours a day in most cases.
- You are comfortable having a stranger live in your home, sharing your kitchen and bathroom.
- You have a plan for backup care should she become ill or unexpectedly leave.

Books About Child Care

The Unofficial Guide to Childcare by Ann Douglas (Wiley, 1998, $15.95).

Au Pairing Up by Ruth K. Liebermann (Musical Press, 2001, $29.95).

The ABCs of Hiring a Nanny by Frances Anne Hernan (McGavick Field, 2000, $19.95).

The Nanny and Domestic Help Legal Kit by J. Alexander Tanford (Sphinx Publishing, 1999, $19.95).

Redbook's Nannies, Au Pairs & Babysitters by Jerri L. Wolfe (Hearst, 2001, $15.95).

141

It is your right to install a hidden nanny-cam in your home if you want to monitor your child's care. For more information about hiring a nanny, visit:

- www.4nanny.com/toughquestions.htm
- www.nanny.org/nannyforfamily.htm

Child Care and Emergency Planning

Create an emergency plan, so that you and your child's caregiver know what to do in the event of an emergency. Discuss how you will reach each other or find each other should something happen. Designate a meeting place if phones do not work. Make sure that your caregiver is committed to caring for your child for an extended time period if there is an emergency and you are unable to get to your child and that she knows how to contact your extended family. Make sure she has an emergency stash of diapers, formula (even if you are breastfeeding, because if you can't get there, the baby still needs to eat), and baby food.

Planning for Maternity Leave

Chapter 5 discussed state disability and employer disability policies during pregnancy. These policies also provide coverage for the postpartum period, for as long as your doctor believes you need to rest or recover. A woman is usually considered "disabled" for six weeks after a vaginal birth and for eight weeks after a C-section birth, but this can vary with a doctor's certification (if your doctor provides written documentation that your birth was somehow out of the ordinary and you need longer to recover). California has a disability leave law that categorizes new parents (including the father or partner) as temporarily disabled, providing payment while he or she cares for a newborn. No other state provides payments for the father or partner.

If you're self-employed, you can use a disability policy you purchased before you became pregnant (see Chapter 1 for information about this).

Family and Medical Leave Act

In addition to time off during pregnancy, you can also use the Family and Medical Leave Act to take time off after your baby's birth. As discussed in Chapter 5, you can take up to twelve weeks of unpaid leave per calendar year and your employer must hold an equivalent position for you (unless you are among the highest-paid 10 percent of employees). You can choose to take this time off as a large chunk, such as the three months after the baby is born, or you can use it to reduce your work hours by working part-time once you return to work. You will need to provide thirty days' notice (notice is not required in emergency situations, so if you should go into labor a month early, you just provide notice as soon as you can), so you should obtain the paperwork now and fill it out. Your human resources contact can hold it so that it can be filed when you want to begin your leave.

Under FMLA, your employer must keep your health benefits in place (but you may have to pay premiums while you are out on maternity leave) and must restore you to your original job or to an equivalent job with equivalent pay when you return. Your employer cannot penalize you for taking the leave or allow it to affect any of your benefits. If you return to work and your employer has taken away some of your job responsibilities or cut your hours, this would be a violation.

If you and your spouse work for the same employer, you are entitled to a total of twelve weeks unpaid FMLA leave, divided between both of you in a twelve-month period, to care for your child. So, for example, you could take ten weeks and your spouse could take two weeks. Your leaves can also be taken simultaneously. The time you take for your own health does not count against your spouse's time, so you could take twelve weeks during pregnancy, and then your spouse could take twelve weeks after the baby is born. Spouses who work for different employers are entitled to each take the full FMLA-allotted twelve weeks. Individual states also have their own pregnancy leave acts, similar to the FMLA. This leave can be combined with FMLA leave to take a larger amount of time off. If you experience any problems with your FMLA request, contact the U.S. Department of Labor at: www.dol.gov.

LEAVE WORKSHEET

Order in Which You Plan to Take Leaves	Type of Leave	Whose Leave? (Yours or Partner's?)	Payment Amount or Percentage	Number of Days Available	Paperwork Completed? (Y/N)

Vacation Time

If your employer offers personal or vacation time, you can use this time in addition to the other time off, if you have accrued it and if you give the required amount of notice. You can be required to use paid vacation time concurrently or prior to your unpaid state or federal FMLA time. If your leave overlaps calendar years, make sure your employer does not require you to use vacation or sick time first in the new year before continuing with FMLA or state pregnancy leave time.

Company-Specific Paid Leave

Some employers offer a certain number of days of paid leave to new mothers or new parents. Inquire of your human resources department what is available. This time usually must be taken after vacation or sick time is used, and because it is full pay, you will want to take it before taking disability or FMLA leave.

Combining Types of Leave

Many women combine disability, vacation time, sick leave, state leave time, and FMLA. Usually you need to take sick and vacation time first. If you have disability leave, it makes sense to take that next, since you will receive disability payments. Save the FMLA leave for last, since that is a leave without pay. To plan your leave, use the worksheet on the previous page.

Managing Paperwork

Start a folder to organize all your leave paperwork and keep copies of everything. Take notes from conversations you have with your human resources contact as well as any phone calls you make to state agencies.

Leave Folder Checklist

- ☐ FMLA application
- ☐ State FMLA application
- ☐ Disability application
- ☐ Vacation time request

☐ Copy of your company's maternity leave policy

☐ Copies of letters or memos to or from your human resources department

☐ Notes about phone calls to HR department or state agencies

☐ A separate set of forms that you will need to ask your health care provider to complete for you once you have the baby, certifying your disability, with stamped and addressed envelopes

☐ A sticky note on the front reminding yourself to make copies of everything before submitting them to anyone

If your partner will also be taking leave time, encourage him or her to assemble a folder with applications, policies, and correspondence as well.

College Leaves

If you are a college or university student, you may decide to take some time off from school. If your baby is due during a semester, it will be difficult to make up classes you've missed. If you do choose to continue in school without a leave, it is important that you talk to your professors and let them know you will be out to have your baby. Many are very understanding and can arrange for you to make up assignments or exams. Your school should have a provision for a medical leave, which will allow you to make up what you have missed once you return. If you are met with resistance and a professor is not willing to accommodate you, speak to the dean of students. If you have a faculty advisor, he or she may be able to offer you some advice but would most likely not be able to intercede on your behalf. If your school has a counseling center, they may be able to offer advice and support, but ultimately, the dean is the only one who can really affect what your professors are doing.

If you do decide to take a leave, apply for it through your dean's office. Do this as soon as you know when you plan to start your leave and once you have decided how long it will last. It is usually not a problem to take a semester leave and then return to complete your degree, but check your school's policy (look in your catalog or contact the dean's office). Complete an application for your leave and list your due date and explain that your leave is for a pregnancy. You may need to provide a letter from your health care provider documenting the pregnancy. If you have a part-time job or a work-study job, notify your employer and inquire if disability pay is available.

College Leave Checklist
☐ Contact the dean of students for information about how to apply for a leave.
☐ Notify professors if you will miss part of a semester, and make arrangements to make up work.
☐ Notify employer of leave and ask about disability pay availability.
☐ Complete school leave application and keep a copy for yourself.
☐ Check impact of leave on scholarships or grants (see page 151).
☐ Have loans placed in deferment (see page 151).

If you are currently in the semester in which your baby is due, you can withdraw from your current courses if you feel you aren't going to be able to complete them. A withdrawal appears on your record, but it does not affect your average (since no grade is given in the course), though it does reduce the credit hours you are given credit for that semester. If it is likely you won't be able to complete the course, a withdrawal may be your best option. You can also take an incomplete for your courses and complete the course require-ments when you return to school, even during another semester. The incomplete appears on your record until you complete the course (and is then changed to your final grade once you complete the course), but it is not as detrimental as a failing grade would be, which is what you will get if you take no action and simply fail to complete the course. Check with your school about their policies.

If your school has an on-site day care, get on the waiting list now if you would like your child to go there. Some schools offer sliding scale rates for students, which can be a substantial savings, as well as convenient.

Your Finances

Paying for Child Care

Child care ends up costing more than most people expect. Take some time now to research your child care options and find out exactly how much each costs. Once you've chosen a method of child care, add the expense to your parenthood budget.

If you pay a nanny (or any other household employee, for that matter) that you have hired yourself (not through an agency, which handles payroll) and pay her more than $1,300 per year, you are required to pay payroll taxes. This includes:

- **Social Security (also called FICA).** Both employer and employee must pay 6.2 percent.
- **Medicare.** Employer and employee must pay 1.45 percent.
- **Federal unemployment tax.** You, the employer, pay .8 percent if you also pay state unemployment tax.
- **State unemployment and disability taxes.** This is paid by both employer and employee.

You will need to obtain an EIN (employer identification number) from the IRS (see IRS Publication #926 at: www.irs.gov). You will also need to file the following forms:

- W-2
- W-3
- SS-4
- Schedule H

W-2 and W-3 forms must be original forms from the IRS (call 800-TAX-FORM) to obtain them. The others can be downloaded from their website (IRS Publication 926 explains how to do this).

If you hire an employee and do not withhold taxes, the Social Security Administration and the IRS can later come back and require you to pay the amounts owed, in addition to interest and fines.

It is against the law to hire an illegal alien, but many people do. If you choose to hire an illegal alien and she later becomes a legal alien, you can be held responsible by the Social Security Administration and the IRS for failing to pay payroll taxes. If you hire a legal alien, you are required to have the employee complete the USCIS (United States Citizenship and Immigration Service) form I-9 (available at: http://uscis.gov/graphics/formsfee/forms/i-9.htm), and you must complete the employer section yourself. You must keep this form on file for three years after the date of hire, or one year after the date of termination, whichever is first.

When you hire a foreigner, verify that he or she is legally in the country. Ask to see the "green card" (resident alien card, permanent alien card, or alien registration receipt card). For help with these documents, see: http://uscis.gov/graphics/services/employer info/oblhome.htm.

Parental Leave and Finances

Although FMLA offers families time to spend with a new baby while maintaining job security, managing the time off without pay can put you in a financial crunch. Likewise, disability leave can also be financially difficult. Not only is the pay reduced, but you may also face processing delays before you receive your checks. To afford a leave, plan ahead.

Now that you have decided about your leave, think about how this is going to impact your household's bottom line. Use the worksheet on the next page to understand what your household income will be in the months after the baby is born, taking into consideration the types of leave and when they run out (refer to the worksheet on page 144).

149
. . .

IMPACT OF LEAVE ON INCOME

Current monthly household income _____
Projected household income Month 1 _____

Total Income Differential Month 1 _____

Current monthly household income _____
Projected household income Month 2 _____

Total Income Differential Month 2 _____

Current monthly household income _____
Projected household income Month 3 _____

Total Income Differential Month 3 _____

Current monthly household income _____
Projected household income Month 4 _____

Total Income Differential Month 4 _____

Current monthly household income _____
Projected household income Month 5 _____

Total Income Differential Month 5 _____

Current monthly household income _____
Projected household income Month 6 _____

Total Income Differential Month 6 _____

Next, compare your monthly projected earnings with your parenthood budget. If your monthly expenses are higher than your projected monthly income, you'll need to find a way to make up this difference.

Dealing with Loans and Scholarships

If you have student loans, scholarships, or grants, consider the implications of taking a leave. Some scholarships and grants continue only if you complete your degree within a certain period of time or if you take a certain number of hours per semester, so check to make sure you will still be eligible. Some scholarships and grants may not apply if you withdraw from your courses, so check those requirements. If you have a Stafford loan or a federal consolidation loan, you can have the loan placed in deferment while you are on leave. This means that you will not have to make payments and the federal government will pay the interest on your loan during this period. You are eligible for a six-month loan deferment if you are pregnant or caring for a child under six months of age. You will need to provide a letter from your health care provider documenting your pregnancy or a copy of the baby's birth certificate, if the deferment will start after the birth.

Dealing with Loans After You Graduate

You are entitled to a loan deferment if you are a working mother with a child not old enough for school and you work full-time in a job that does not pay more than $1 above minimum wage. You must provide your pay stub and a copy of the child's birth certificate. To obtain a copy of the form you need in order to request a deferment, contact your school's financial aid office.

If you use up this deferment period (a maximum of six months for parental leave for federal loans) and will not be returning to school or are finished with school, you can request a forbearance, which is a reduction in payments, a complete hold on payments, or an extension of payment deadlines. To qualify, show economic hardship by proving that you do not work full-time and your monthly income is not more than twice the federal minimum wage or is not more than twice the poverty line for a family of two in your state (you can find this information online at: www.ssc.wisc.edu/irp, or by contacting your lender). You can also claim hardship if you work full-time and your total student loan payments are greater or equal to 20 percent of your monthly income. Obtain a copy of the request for forbearance from your school's financial aid office or from your lender.

For more information on student loans, see:

- Stafford Loans at: www.staffordloan.com
- National Student Loan Data Center at: www.nslds.ed.gov

Your Lifestyle

Traveling During the Third Trimester

The biggest concern about traveling in your third trimester is going into preterm labor and not having access to your doctor, hospital, or family. If you're not at high risk, it may be safe to travel by plane until the last month, but discuss this with your health care provider. The pressurized cabin of an airplane usually poses no great risk to you or your baby (but again, check with your health care provider). Metal detectors are not dangerous for you or your baby. The biggest issue is usually comfort. Follow these tips when traveling by airplane:

- Pack an inflatable pillow or a blanket that you can roll up and place behind your back or neck.
- Do not carry heavy luggage (pulling rolling luggage may be OK, but ask your health care provider) or try to lift luggage into the overhead compartment of an airplane or into a car.
- Drink plenty of water and eat regularly.
- Ask for an aisle seat so you can get to the bathroom easily.
- Try not to sit in one position for too long, and walk, stretch, and move as much as possible to help avoid blood clots and discomfort.

When you travel, take a copy of your medical records with you and have your health care provider's phone number with you. You should also carry a letter from your health care provider that gives your due date. Many airlines will not allow pregnant women to travel if they are within a month of their due date, so have documentation with you in case there is a question. Each airline has its own requirements. Check your airline's website or call their 800 number to get information.

Most travel insurance companies do not provide travel insurance during the last two months of pregnancy, so if you do travel, you will probably not be able to buy travel insurance.

If you travel by train, find out where the train stops and how often. If you travel by car, map out your trip and pinpoint hospitals along the way in case you need care. You might also consider purchasing OnStar service (www.OnStar.com), which has a cell phone built into your car. Representatives are always available, can pinpoint your exact location, and can tell you how to get to the nearest hospital or they can send emergency personnel to you. As with air travel, stretch and move around so that you keep good blood flow going to your legs. It is best to avoid cruise ships in the last month of pregnancy (or earlier if you are having any kind of problem) because of the length of time it would take to get to a hospital. If you do take a cruise, find out how quickly you could be transported to a hospital.

When planning travel, call your health insurance company and find out what kind of coverage you have for out-of-town care. Most health insurance companies can give you a twenty-four-hour hotline number to call to find out where to go in an emergency.

Fill your prescriptions before you go. Take the prescription bottles with you instead of placing medication in a pill dispenser. If you are questioned about what the pill is, you will have the bottle, showing the prescription and the contact information for the drugstore if there is any question. This will provide accurate dosage information should you need medical attention while you are away.

153

Considering Labor Software

Computer programs are available to help you track your labor using a Palm or other pocket computer. If you're interested in one of these programs, download it now and practice using it so you are familiar with it.

• **Labor Coach.** This $20 program for Palm and other hand-held units tracks contractions and allows you to enter in milestones such as your water breaking or contraction intensity. The program will output graphs of your contractions. Find it at: http://shop.store .yahoo.com/pilotgearsw/laborcoach.html.

• **Contraction Timer.** This free program lets you track contractions and make notes using your Palm or other handheld unit. The program calculates the time between contractions and their duration and beeps when they are less than three minutes apart. Find it at: www.freewarepalm.com/medical/contractiontimer.shtml.

• **Pregnancy Assistant.** This $10 download for Palm OS calculates your due date and indicates where you currently are in your pregnancy. It will also time contractions and calculate the length of and interval between them. You can set an alarm to go off when your contractions reach a threshold determined by your health care provider, alerting you that it's time to go to the hospital or birth center. It also stores and displays your health care provider's phone number. Find it at: www.arkelproducts.com/software.html.

Registering for Classes

There are a variety of classes, beyond labor and delivery preparation and sibling classes, available for expectant parents. You might be interested in classes about:

• Breastfeeding
• Infant CPR
• Baby care
• Childproofing
• Infant massage

Contact your insurance company and find out if any of these classes are covered and, if so, ask for a list. If these classes are not covered but you are still interested, contact the hospital or birth center where you plan to have your baby and ask if they offer any or can recommend any. Be sure to add the cost of the classes to your pregnancy budget.

Month 7 Checklist

☐ Interview and choose a pediatrician.
☐ Consider day care options and interview potential caregivers.
☐ Create a child care emergency plan.
☐ Plan what kind of leave you will take from work after the baby is born.
☐ Plan a college leave if you are a student.
☐ Plan how to afford your leave.
☐ Plan for child care expenses.
☐ Obtain paperwork for student loan deferments.
☐ Revise your parenthood budget.
☐ Obtain a letter from your health care provider before flying, and consider where you would obtain emergency care while out of town and what your insurance coverage would be.
☐ Consider labor software.
☐ Register for classes.

9

Month 8

C heyenne and her husband hired a nanny. They decided not to go to the trouble of withholding payroll tax. The nanny used their car to drive their children around on errands, to the park, and to activities. One day she had a small accident while driving the car. In the police report she explained she was a full-time nanny. The children were perfectly OK, but the insurance company refused to pay for the damage because the nanny was an employee, not a guest driver. Cheyenne and her husband had to pay for the accident themselves. If they had added her to the policy, the accident would have been covered.

You know you're getting close when month eight comes around. You're starting to feel huge and tired and are ready to make final preparations, so that when that baby comes along you are prepared. You also should feel a real sense of accomplishment. After all, you've made it this far and you're in the home stretch. This is a good time to firm up your maternity leave plans, buy a camera or video camera, and prepare some meals in advance.

Your Rights

Your Rights in a Hospital

If you're planning to give birth in a hospital, you might be feeling a little uncomfortable at the thought of having to be a hospital patient. For many women, childbirth is their first hospital stay. It's important to remember that a hospital is a bureaucracy with rules and regulations, as well as a place designed to care for you and your baby. Before you stay in a hospital, it's important to understand your rights while you are there.

For a basic overview of your rights, read the American Hospital Association's Patient's Bill of Rights at: www.hospitalconnect .com/aha/ptcommunication/partnership/index.html.

Informed Consent

The concept of informed consent was discussed in Chapter 3. Informed consent rules apply to your care during your hospital stay. So many things are routine in a hospital that the people providing the care often don't think about the fact that the treatment they are providing is new to you. For this reason, it's important that you always ask if you have questions or don't understand something. It is your absolute right to have a procedure or treatment explained to you, and it doesn't matter how rushed the staff is or how many other things they need to do. If you need information, they must provide it.

Confidentiality

Hospitals are required to follow the Health Insurance Portability and Accountability Act (HIPAA; see Chapter 2) to protect a patient's privacy. You have the right to access your hospital medical records, and copies of all records must be provided within thirty days of your request. The hospital cannot share your information with anyone without your permission, so they cannot tell your employer you had a C-section, leave a message with your mother that your bill is overdue, or use your case in a marketing campaign to show what great care they offer women with gestational diabetes. The hospital must take reasonable steps to protect your medical privacy, although this can be problematic when you have a roommate. You should be able to discuss your medical concerns without anyone overhearing. All hospitals have private exam rooms and you can ask to be examined or have a conversation with your health care provider there.

You must be given the right to opt out of being listed in the hospital's directory (a public listing of patients that not only lists who is staying there but also describes patients' conditions, with general terms like critical, stable, or good).

Hospital Personnel

Confidentiality applies to all hospital personnel, including the following:

- **Intern.** An intern is a medical student who has received training and is able to see patients in a supervised capacity. You will only encounter an intern if you are going to a teaching hospital. If you do not wish to be seen by an intern, you can simply say so.
- **Resident.** A resident is a medical school graduate who is gaining experience in his or her chosen specialty field. Residents can provide treatment and prescribe medications for patients. They are supervised by the medical staff, but for practical purposes, they sometimes may be the only doctor available to deal with an emergency or problem that comes up. If you do not wish to be treated by a resident, your only option is to wait until your health care provider is available, and it may be a long wait if he or she is attending births.
- **Staff physician.** Although your health care provider is the person truly in charge of your treatment, a staff physician will provide care when your health care provider is not available (for example, if she is delivering another baby). Again, you can insist on waiting for your own provider, but if you need treatment immediately, it makes no sense to refuse to allow the staff physician to provide your care.
- **Registered nurse.** A registered nurse is also called an RN. There are different types of maternity RNs—those who specialize in helping women through labor and delivery; RNs who specialize

in working on the maternity ward, caring for women after birth; and RNs who work in the newborn nursery. RNs can administer medication and are in charge of supervising your and your baby's actual care.

• **Nurse practitioner.** This is a nurse with a master's degree and additional experience. They often are in charge of supervising care, such as in the nursery.

• **Licensed practical nurse.** Also known as an LPN, this kind of nurse handles daily care, such as changing bandages, helping you to the bathroom, taking your temperature and blood pressure, and assisting you with personal care.

• **Lactation specialist or consultant.** This is a nurse who has received extra training in lactation, or breastfeeding. She can help you with problems such as getting the baby to nurse, painful breasts, pumping, and the different holds that might work for you. Ask to see one if you are breastfeeding.

• **Perinatologist.** This is an obstetrician who specializes in high-risk pregnancies (also called a Maternal-Fetal Medicine Specialist). Your physician may consult with one or may turn your care over to one, depending on the seriousness of the problem.

• **Neonatologist.** This is a pediatrician specializing in the care of newborns. This type of doctor provides care for newborns in the nursery. You would not normally see this type of doctor in the delivery room unless there is an anticipated problem.

• **Anesthesiologist.** This is a physician who provides epidurals, spinals, and general anesthetic. This type of physician is on staff at the hospital and is available to provide treatment, whether or not you have included pain management in your birth plan.

• **Nurse anesthetist.** This is a nurse who has special training in anesthesiology and monitors your pain.

• **Patient advocate.** Patient advocates work to make sure hospital patients receive the care they need and are satisfied. One may come to your room and check to make sure everything has gone all right. If you do encounter a problem while you are in the hospital and cannot get it resolved on your own (for example, a nurse does not respond to your call button despite repeated attempts), call the administration offices of your hospital (or send a friend or family member down in person) and a patient advocate will be in touch with you to help resolve the problem.

Drive-Through Delivery Laws
Several years ago insurance companies were pressuring hospitals to get women out of the hospital more quickly after delivery. Some women were discharged within hours after delivery and went home to experience problems themselves or discover a problem with the baby. In response to this, thirty-two states enacted laws and a federal law was put into place that requires insurers to pay for a forty-eight-hour stay after a normal vaginal delivery and a ninety-six-hour stay after a C-section delivery. In Maryland, if the mother feels she needs to stay longer, the insurer must pay. In other states, if you wish to stay longer, you need to discuss this with your health care provider, who can then persuade the insurer that a longer stay is needed.

If your insurer does not pay for an extended stay, you can appeal its decision. The patient advocate at your hospital can assist you in appealing the decision, and there may be an insurance specialist in the hospital as well who can assist you. If you wish to leave the hospital sooner than the minimum stay, discuss this with your health care provider. When possible, this should be a mutual decision so that you are not leaving against medical advice (AMA, see Chapter 5).

Circumcision

161

If you have a boy, your health care provider will ask you if you would like to have the baby circumcised. This choice is completely up to you. The American Academy of Pediatrics does not believe that there is enough evidence to recommend circumcision of all boys, although there are some studies that show a lower risk of certain infections and problems among circumcised boys. Circumcision is a type of surgery, and you have the right to request that your son be given pain relief. The obstetrician, not the pediatrician, does circumcisions, so talk with your obstetrician about the procedure and how it is performed. Circumcision cannot be performed unless you sign a consent form.

Read about the circumcision choice at: www.aap.org/healthtop ics/Stages.cfm#inf.

Newborn Testing

Your hospital or birth center is required by your state to perform certain tests to make sure your newborn is as perfect as he or she appears. These tests check for hereditary abnormalities. They are tested for at birth because often the sooner a problem is identified, the sooner it can be treated. These abnormalities cannot be tested for while you are pregnant because it is the baby's blood that must be tested and not your amniotic fluid, your blood, or the images on an ultrasound. Some parents feel helpless or frightened when they learn that their baby will be tested for problems they may never have even heard of, but these tests are just precautions. If your baby were to have a problem, the sooner it is discovered, the faster treatment can begin. Each state has its own laws about which tests are required. To find out what disorders are screened for in your state, visit: www.savebabies.org/NBS/statenbsprogramreport .php. The disparity between states is wide, with some states screening for only four conditions and others screening for forty-eight.

Even though your state may not require complete screening, you are entitled to have your child screened completely. For under $90 you can have your child screened for all conditions recommended by the Save Babies Through Screening Foundation (www.savebabies .org). This organization lists labs that will do complete testing. Contact a lab and purchase the sampling kit from them. Order the screening packet before delivery and take it with you to the hospital. The hospital nursery staff will take the samples necessary for the screening. Only a few extra drops of blood are needed and they can be collected during the same heel stick procedure as is done for your state tests, so no additional needles are necessary. The cost of additional testing will not be covered by your health insurance, unless there is a family history of certain illnesses and your pediatrician orders the tests. Test results will be provided to you and to your pediatrician if you authorize it.

In some states it is possible to opt out of the state-required screening, and some parents choose to do so because it is upsetting to see your infant's heel stuck with a needle (if your baby is rooming-in, this test is often performed in your room) to produce the drops of blood necessary for testing. However, the discomfort is small when weighed against the important information you may gain. In other states you can only refuse testing because of religious beliefs. If you are considering not having your child tested, find out what the requirements in your state are. Discuss this with your pediatrician. If you opt out of the testing at birth, these tests would not be performed again at any stage in your child's life, unless your pediatrician later suspected some problem.

The American Speech-Language-Hearing Association (ASHA) recommends that all newborns be tested for hearing loss using a noninvasive, painless procedure. Thirty-seven states have laws requiring hearing screening. For more information and to find out about your state law, see: www.asha.org. If your state does not automatically screen for this, you can request that your baby be tested for a problem, but it may not be covered by your insurance and the test may have to be done at an audiologist's office if the hospital or your pediatrician does not have the right equipment.

Your baby will be evaluated in the delivery room using Apgar scores. The Apgar scoring system evaluates the baby's appearance at one minute and five minutes after birth in five categories: respiration and crying, reflexes and irritability, pulse and heart rate, skin color of body and extremities, and muscle tone. Scores for each category are 0, 1, or 2, with 2 being the highest and most desirable. Talk to your pediatrician for an interpretation of your baby's scores.

163
. . .

Checking for Recalls

Safety standards change over the years, and products are recalled. If you own used baby equipment or furniture, it pays to do a little research to make sure it will be safe for your baby. You can check all recalls of consumer products through the U.S. Consumer Product Safety Commission site at: www.cpsc.gov. Recalls dating back to 1973 are listed on the site.

To find out if a product meets current safety standards, check the Juvenile Product Manufacturer's Association website at: www .jpma.org. The consumer section of the site contains a complete room-by-room listing of safety guidelines for all baby products. Read the guidelines and make sure that any used items you are planning to use conform to the current safety requirements.

Reconsidering Changes in Your Work Schedule

Although you might have decided earlier in your pregnancy that you didn't want to take time off during your pregnancy, you might be finding now that it is harder for you to continue with the same activities or schedules. If you're feeling overwhelmed or extremely uncomfortable, think about what you can do to make yourself more comfortable and make your last month of pregnancy go smoothly.

You might be able to make some changes that are minor, such as getting a more comfortable work chair or arranging things so you don't need to stand as much. Cutting back work hours or choosing to stop working completely may be an option. If you're experiencing discomfort at work, discuss this with your health care provider, who can help you find possible solutions and can make recommendations about how much you should be doing.

It can't hurt to ask again about reduced hours, flextime, or job sharing, even if you got a resounding no earlier in your pregnancy. If you need to reduce your hours or go on leave for medical reasons, your employer must comply. See Chapter 5 for more information about leave during pregnancy. Be sure to discuss your decision with your health care provider. If, for example, you are experiencing Braxton Hicks contractions or ankle swelling, he or she might provide you with documentation for disability or a letter to your employer explaining that you can no longer perform certain duties.

Dealing with Commuting

If you are experiencing discomfort during your commute, look for ways to stay comfortable. If you ride public transportation, ask people to give up their seats for you (when you are obviously pregnant, few people will have a problem with this). You can drive a car as long as your provider says it's OK, which for most women is until they deliver. Be sure to place your seat belt under your uterus and adjust the seat and steering wheel if necessary to accommodate your size.

If you are having difficulty walking from your car to your place of business (or into stores), talk to your provider about a handicap parking tag. To qualify, your provider will need to certify to the state motor vehicles department that you are temporarily disabled. Many stores now have expectant mother parking, spaces labeled as intended for pregnant women.

Your Finances

Flexible Spending Accounts (FSAs) and Child Care Credit

Medical flexible spending accounts were discussed in Chapter 2. Flexible spending accounts are also available for child care expenses. If your child will be going to day care or you will be employing a nanny or sitter, you should consider setting up an FSA. If your employer offers an FSA, you can have up to $5,000 taken out of your pay, pretax, and placed in a flexible spending account. Five thousand dollars is the family limit and is the total that you and your spouse can set aside combined. You can then use this money to pay for your child care expenses without paying tax on it.

The need for child care must be so that you or your spouse can work or look for work. You cannot claim payments made while you are out sick or on maternity leave. You can include money paid to a relative who is providing child care for you. Funds not used within a calendar year are forfeited. When you claim this money, you must be able to provide the child care giver's taxpayer ID number. Get receipts or keep copies of cashed checks so that you have evidence of what you paid.

You can start to save money into an FSA while you are pregnant, but be sure you will have day care expenses. If you have the baby and then decide that you or your partner will be staying home to care for the baby full-time, you will lose the money you saved.

There is another way to use child care expenses to decrease your tax bill. You can claim the child care credit (IRS Publication 503 at: www.irs.gov), which is a deduction of about 20 percent of the amount you spend on child care. To claim this credit on your tax return you must use form 1040 or 1040A (you can't use form 1040EZ). You can claim up to $3,000 in expenses for one child and $6,000 for two children. You cannot take both the FSA and the child care credit, though. Any money you put in an FSA is subtracted from what you are claiming on your child care credit. Talk to your tax preparer about which choice will benefit your situation more—it usually makes more sense to max out your FSA first before taking the child care credit. This online calculator can calculate your tax savings if you use an FSA: http://kiplinger.com/tools/flex.

To decide which option works best for you, look at your tax return to determine your tax rate. If your tax rate is higher than 20 percent (the savings you get with the child care credit) you are probably better off using an FSA, because the child care money is taken out of your pay tax free, meaning you save the entire percent you are taxed at for that chunk of money.

Reviewing Your Insurance

If you will be hiring a nanny or sitter who will be driving your vehicle, review your auto insurance policy. If an accident occurs with your vehicle, your insurance provides coverage, even if you are not driving the vehicle. However, if your nanny will be driving your car on a regular basis, add her on as an additional driver, so there can be no question should an accident happen. Note that the insurance rate for each car is based on the person driving it who has the worst record. So if you have a perfect record and you add a nanny who has had some accidents, the rate is going to go up. If you hire a nanny from an agency, she is employed by them and is just a guest driver and would be covered without you doing anything extra. However, if she will be driving the car on a regular basis, your insurance company might still require that you notify them. Check with your insurance agent.

If your nanny will be transporting your child in her car, she needs to obtain a rider, since any accident involving the children would be considered an "on the job" occurrence. You, as the employer, should offer to pay this additional premium.

If your nanny is injured on your property, your homeowner's insurance policy may not provide coverage, since she is technically an employee. To be completely safe, hire your nanny legally so that state workers' compensation insurance would cover any injuries. If you do not have coverage and she is somehow injured on your property, you would be responsible for the medical bills and possibly for lost wages, and you might end up liable for civil and criminal penalties for failing to withhold taxes and pay workers' compensation payments to your state. If you hire a nanny from an agency, she is employed by the agency and is a guest in your home and would be covered by your policy. Add additional payments for insurance to your parenthood budget.

Your Lifestyle

Buying a Camera

A good camera is a must-have for new parents. You'll want to get some great shots of your new baby on the hospital scale, with the funny little beanie cap on, and snuggled in your arms for the very first time. As new parents, you will want a camera that is easy to use, pretty foolproof, and very reliable. You don't want to be fumbling around in the delivery room with buttons and settings, and you want to be sure that when you've taken a photo that it will turn out, otherwise you've lost that precious moment.

Camera Shopping Tips

Go to local stores and actually hold and try out the cameras you are considering. Find out if there are any rebates or special packages available. Consider features such as memory space, auto focus, battery life, and zoom. Compare prices at local stores as well as online. The website: www.MySimon.com will do a price comparison for you among online retailers. Be sure to adjust your pregnancy budget when you buy a camera. If you will be using a 35mm camera, add the cost of film and developing to your parenthood budget.

Tips for Using Cameras

You and your partner should learn how to use the camera now so that you are fully prepared in the delivery room. Take photos, try out all the features, and download photos to your computer now so that you are skilled at it. Practice adjusting, cropping, and editing photos and attaching them to e-mails or burning them to a CD now. Buy more memory (or film) than you think you will need and bring it to the hospital. Don't leave the camera unattended in your hospital room. Have your partner wear it into the delivery room and take it home if he or she goes home to sleep.

For more information about choosing a camera, go to: www .shortcourses.com/choosing/contents.htm.

Choosing a Video Camera

You may decide you also want a video camera, and if you do, experts suggest that you purchase it separately and not buy a combination still/video camera. Digital video cameras range from $400 to $3,000. Make sure the camera allows you to download to your computer. A camera with optical stabilization will keep the images stable. The higher the pixels, the better the resolution. Buy extra batteries, so that when one dies, you've got another ready to go. If your camera records onto DVD, make sure you buy plenty of DVDs. Always label the DVDs so that you will know what is stored on them.

Using Your Video Camera

Practice using your video camera before the baby is born. Learn not to zoom in and out too frequently. Learn what kind of lighting produces the best shots with your camera and make sure you are always shooting with enough light. Take shots from various angles for variety. Your videos will be more viewable if you take short clips instead of long ones.

Preparing Meals in Advance

In the weeks after the baby is born, cooking is going to be one of the last things on your mind. Now is the time to start to lay in a supply of frozen meals that can be reheated. One easy way to create frozen meals is to double the recipe when you cook your daily meals and freeze half. Some people find that they can freeze a lot of meals if they take one day and cook several things.

Dishes that freeze well include:

- Casseroles
- Lasagna and pasta dishes
- Soup
- Taco meat and enchiladas
- Stews
- Meat loaf
- Quiche

Do a big grocery shopping trip (have your partner deal with loading and unloading the bags) and stock up on items that are easy to make so that they will be on hand once the baby comes. These include:

- Canned vegetables
- Canned fruit
- Frozen vegetables
- Frozen pizza
- Loaves of bread (to freeze so they won't get stale)
- Rolls (to freeze)
- Instant rice
- Cans of soup
- A few premade frozen dinners or entrées
- Bottled juice or frozen concentrate
- Extra condiments
- Granola bars
- Boxes of cereal or oatmeal
- Bagels or muffins to freeze

Getting Ready for Your Shower

If you will be having a baby shower, there are some things you can do beforehand to help you stay organized. Get a copy of the guest list and create address labels for each guest on your computer. This will make writing thank-you notes much easier. You might also consider asking the person who is hosting the shower to create these labels for you. She can use them for the invitations as well.

If you do not have preprinted address labels for yourself, this is a good time to order them, since you will need them for shower gifts as well as birth announcements, christening invitations, and thank-you notes after the baby is born.

Take the log on pages 171–172 with you to your shower and ask a friend to fill it out as you are opening gifts, so you can keep track of who gave you what. If you have more than one shower planned, photocopy this blank log to keep track of additional gifts.

SHOWER GIFT LOG

Name of Gift Giver	Item	Date Thank-You Sent
_____	_____	_____
_____	_____	_____
_____	_____	_____
_____	_____	_____
_____	_____	_____
_____	_____	_____
_____	_____	_____
_____	_____	_____
_____	_____	_____
_____	_____	_____
_____	_____	_____
_____	_____	_____
_____	_____	_____
_____	_____	_____
_____	_____	_____
_____	_____	_____
_____	_____	_____

Name of Gift Giver	Item	Date Thank-You Sent

When you open the gifts, tuck the cards into the gifts so that if something was not recorded on your list you'll be able to figure out who it is from. Add the cost of thank-you notes to your pregnancy budget.

Organizing the Nursery

If you haven't already gotten the nursery put together, now is the time to do so. The easiest way to plan out the room is to use graph paper. Take measurements of all the walls, as well as the windows and doors. Plot out a diagram of the room on graph paper. A scale of one foot or six inches per square will probably work well. Then cut out the crib, dresser, and other furniture from another piece of graph paper, using the same scale. Move the cutouts around on the diagram to see how they best fit. It is much easier to move pieces of paper around than it is to move furniture.

Learning About Choking Hazards

You probably already know that babies can choke on small objects, but it can be hard to gauge what is safe and what isn't. You can't rely on manufacturers to always provide completely safe products. Consider purchasing a choke test cylinder. This small clear plastic tube is the size of a child's throat. If something fits in the tube, it's too small for your baby. Having this inexpensive item on hand can give you an easy way to test the safety of toys and household objects. Find one at your local baby store.

173

Month 8 Checklist
- [ ] Educate yourself about the circumcision decision.
- [ ] Find out what newborn screening tests are required in your state.
- [ ] Purchase additional newborn screening tests if you are interested.
- [ ] Check for recalls and safety requirements on any used baby products you plan on using.

- ☐ Reassess whether you will be able to continue working to the end of your pregnancy and consider options if you feel you won't be able to.
- ☐ Ask for a handicap parking tag if you need one.
- ☐ Consider whether you need an FSA for child care and get one set up if you do.
- ☐ Consider your insurance needs if you will be hiring a nanny.
- ☐ Comparison shop for a camera and/or video camera.
- ☐ Freeze meals and stock your pantry.
- ☐ Prepare a gift log to use at your shower and consider creating address labels.
- ☐ Do a scale drawing of the nursery and try out furniture arrangements.
- ☐ Learn about choking hazards.

Month 9

Anita was ready for her baby to arrive, but she was beginning to think she didn't want to return to work full-time to her graphic designer job after the birth. Anita talked to a coworker who recently had a baby and they put together a job sharing proposal to present to their manager. Anita worked on the presentation and created an organized document that neatly and concisely presented their plan. The other mom had health insurance through her spouse. Anita and her partner compared their health insurance plans and decided that Anita's family plan saved them more money, so she included health insurance for one employee in her plan. She and the other mom agreed to split Anita's current salary

This is it—your last month! One more month of tentlike clothing, constant bathroom trips, and feeling ready to pop. The first thing to remember to do during your last month of pregnancy is to enjoy it—as tired as you are of being pregnant, it will soon be over. This month you'll want to get your bag ready to go to the hospital or birth center, discuss C-sections with your health care provider, and firm up your work schedule for after the baby's arrival.

and each work two and a half days. Anita's employer agreed to the plan, and she was able to spend time at home with her baby while keeping her job and her health insurance.

Your Rights

Planning a New Work Schedule for You and Your Partner

You're going to be parents soon and it's time to think in detail about how you and your partner are going to manage your work schedules after the baby comes and your leave time is over. There are a variety of options available.

Part-Time

You might consider changing your hours to part-time after the baby is born. This way you will still have a job but will have more time to be with your baby. Your employer may be able to offer you a reduction in hours, or you may need to think about looking elsewhere. It is likely that you won't get health insurance benefits, though, if you work part-time, so this is something to consider.

Flextime

Your (or your partner's) employer may offer official or unofficial flextime. Official flextime allows you to work the same number of hours but at the times you choose, as long as you formally report it. Ask for your employer's written policy on flextime. You may be required to structure your schedule so that you are still working no more and no less than forty hours a week so your employer complies with overtime laws. Informal flextime happens when you have a job where you can take work home, come in early, leave early, or do things over the weekend and often works best for salaried employees.

Flextime will allow you to arrange your schedule around your baby's schedule. At the time this book was written, there were plans to change labor regulations, allowing workers to take time off as compensation for overtime instead of getting overtime pay; however, this legislation has not yet been implemented. If you are considering using flextime:

- Get your company's written policy.
- Talk to other employees in your office who have used flextime and find out how it worked for them.
- Think about how the schedule will impact your ability to work. For example, will it be difficult to communicate with other employees if you are not there when they are?
- Create a written proposal or plan.

Job Sharing

Job sharing is not as popular as it once was, but it is still a possibility in some companies. If you're thinking about job sharing, you're more likely to succeed if you can find a coworker who also wants to job share and then present a complete plan to your employer. Choose someone who is reliable. In addition to sharing job responsibilities, you will be sharing a salary, so include this pay reduction in your parenthood budget.

When considering a job sharing arrangement:

- Create a written proposal.
- Do not say why you want to do this (the why is irrelevant).
- Create a job sharing plan that will highlight your abilities and make the most of them.
- Make sure your plan incorporates all of your current job responsibilities.
- Try to word your plan so that it appears to fit in with your company's mission.
- Find out if you will still be eligible for health insurance.

Independent Contracting

You may be able to fill a similar role for your employer as an independent contractor, allowing you to set your own hours and be more flexible. However, this means setting up your own business and paying your own taxes. Giving up health insurance is an important concern as well, but you may be able to get a family rate through your spouse's health insurance or purchase your own through a local chamber of commerce. Consider what to do about your retirement plan. If you are self-employed, you are able to set up a 401K or IRA for yourself. Talk to your financial advisor for more information. Consider the following when evaluating independent contracting:

- How much will you save on commuting?
- How much will it cost to set up a home office?
- How comfortable are you working without a set salary?
- Are there potential clients for your service other than your current employer?
- How will you work from home and care for your child? Factor in needed child care expenses.
- How willing will your employer be to hire you as an independent contractor?
- Will you be able to generate enough business and income to compensate for the costs of paying your own taxes?

Talking About Birth Options

As your delivery draws nearer, ask last-minute questions of your health care provider. If you are seriously considering a home birth, find out whether your provider feels this is a good option for you based on what has happened so far in your pregnancy. You should also finalize your birth plan and give a copy of it to your health care provider.

Ask About C-Sections

Even if you plan on having a vaginal birth, a C-section could become necessary, and it's helpful to be prepared for any eventuality by gathering information now, since you won't have a lot of time to ask questions if one becomes necessary. You will be asked to sign a separate consent form for this surgery if it is necessary for you. Have your partner read the form—you'll be in labor and may not be able to concentrate very well. If you have a midwife, an obstetrician would be called in to do the surgery.

Ask your health care provider these questions about C-sections now:

- What kind of anesthesia she recommends
- If you are using a midwife, which obstetrician would do the surgery
- When a C-section would be necessary and how the determination would be made
- What the recovery is like
- How long you would stay in the hospital
- How the surgery is performed
- Whether stitches or staples are used to close the incision
- Who can be with you during the surgery and when he or she can come in the room
- When you will get to see your baby after the surgery
- How long you would have to stay in the hospital
- What the risks are to you and the baby

Ask about the type of incision that would be made. Your health care provider will most likely explain to you that a horizontal incision is almost always used, since this heals more easily and decreases the risk of rupture in later pregnancies. The other type of incision is a vertical incision, which is only used in rare emergency situations. However, it is important that you make your preference for a horizontal incision known.

If you do have a C-section, insist that you be given a catheter *after* your epidural or spinal so that you do not feel it. If you have problems with nausea after surgery or a family history of this, be sure to tell your doctor and anesthesiologist. If you have concerns during the surgery, raise them. The entire team is there to take care of you and you should speak up if you have worries or questions. The nurses in the operating room will provide emotional support if you need it and will also probably offer to take photos of you and your partner with the new baby if you would like.

When you go to the recovery room after the surgery, speak up if you are experiencing discomfort or if you are cold. Your partner can be with you in recovery. Your baby will most likely go to the nursery while you are there, but your partner can go check in on the baby any time. Ask your health care provider about hospital policies for C-sections.

Choosing an Elective C-Section

If you want a scheduled C-section, talk to your health care provider. He or she may try to talk you out of it or simply explain that he or she does not do this type of surgery (although this is rare). Scheduled C-sections are generally covered by health insurance, but you should check with your health care provider to make sure yours will be. Your insurance company can also help you determine this.

Books About C-Sections

The Essential C-Section Guide by Maureen Connolly (Broadway, 2004, $14.00).

Cesarean Recovery by Chrissie Gallagher-Mundy (Firefly, 2004, $19.95).

Cesarean Section: Understanding and Celebrating Your Baby's Birth by Michele Moore (Johns Hopkins University Press, 2003, $14.95).

What If I Have a C-Section? by Rita Rubin (Rodale, 2004, $12.95).

Completing Preadmission Paperwork

If you are planning a hospital birth, go to the hospital to complete preadmission paperwork in your ninth month. This is so that when you are in labor you won't have to bother with forms and insurance information. When you do your preadmission paperwork you will be asked to provide your insurance card and fill out forms on which you indicate your address, date of birth, next of kin, allergies, and other medical conditions. You will also be asked to sign a consent form (see Chapter 6 for more information), which will allow the hospital and staff to treat you while you are there. Read the consent form so that you understand what you are agreeing to. When you do this paperwork, you will also be asked if you have a health care directive and, if so, where it is kept. If you do not have one, the hospital can provide you with a basic form to use (although it is important to understand that this form often does not fully explain your wishes and so it is best to have your own document drawn up beforehand; see Chapter 7 for more information). Bring your health insurance card and a copy of your birth plan.

Have someone drive you to the hospital to fill out the preadmission paperwork. Hospital parking lots are large and often quite full and there may be no convenient parking. If you can be dropped off at the door it will make things easier for you. While you are there find out where to enter the hospital if you go into labor at night. Where should you park? Is there a different door to use at night? Do you go directly to the maternity ward or do you check in elsewhere?

Car Seat Laws

All fifty states require that children up to age eighteen months ride in a car seat, with many states extending that requirement to age four. Some states require booster seats for older children. A car seat is the only way to make sure your child remains safe while riding in a car. You should install your car seat now so that when your baby is born it will be ready and waiting. If you give birth at a hospital you may not be allowed to leave unless you place your child in a car seat.

Using a car seat is important, but if it isn't installed correctly, your baby won't be completely protected. Carefully follow the instructions that come with your car seat and consider taking your car to a car seat inspection station. A list of some stations sponsored by the National Safe Kids Campaign is available online at: www.safekids.org/tier2_rl.cfm?folder_id=1400, or by calling 202-662-0600. Local police and sheriff departments also often hold car seat safety days, so check your local paper or call your local police department for information. As of September 1, 2002, the LATCH system (Lower Anchors and Tethers for Children) is now required in new vehicles and on new car seats. The law requires vehicles to have a special built-in latch for the car seat to attach to. This system is designed to make car seat installation easier and safer. If you aren't sure if your vehicle has this system, try installing the car seat using the LATCH instructions that came with it. If you are unable to install it according to the LATCH instructions, call your car manufacturer's customer service number and ask if your model has the LATCH system and, if so, how to use it. Go to an inspection station to have your installation checked by professionals.

If your car seat has a detachable infant carrier, practice detaching it and reattaching it now. Use a stuffed animal or five small rolled-up towels (one for each arm and leg and one for the abdomen) and practice latching the seat belt. It's much easier to learn to do this now than when you're leaving the hospital and there is a crying baby in the seat.

A recent case in the news put the spotlight on breastfeeding while driving, when a Michigan woman was pulled over for breastfeeding while she was driving. She was later convicted of child endangerment. Some states (notably Michigan, which was involved in the case) have laws that provide an exception to car seat laws while an infant is being breastfed, but the intent of the laws is to allow breastfeeding by a passenger, not a driver. It is never safe (and no state makes it legal) to breastfeed and drive at the same time. If you are not the driver, your state may allow you to remove the infant from the car seat for breastfeeding, but it is important to realize the risk you are taking with the baby's safety. Should you be in an accident, you cannot protect him or her as well as the child safety seat can.

Read your state's car seat laws online at: www.inventiveparent .com/state-laws.htm.

Your Finances

Adding a Baby to Your Health Insurance Policy
Find out what you need to do to add your baby to your health insurance policy. The birth of a child is a qualifying event and allows you to change your coverage from individual to family upon the date of the baby's birth. This change is done automatically when the birth is reported by the hospital to the health insurance company. If your baby will not be on your policy but instead will be on your partner's, be sure to notify the hospital when you do your preadmission paperwork.

If you and your spouse each have individual policies, determine what it will cost to change one of those policies to a family policy when the baby is born. Also, weigh the coverage each policy provides and ask about co-pays for pediatric visits, since your child will be having regular well-baby visits. Then, factor in prescription plan coverage and co-pays. Use the worksheet on the next page to help you compare the policies.

If you and your partner are both on the same policy, then you already have a family policy. The health insurance company will automatically add the baby once he or she is born and the hospital notifies them, and there will be no additional cost to add the baby to the policy.

183
···

HEALTH INSURANCE COMPARISON WORKSHEET

	Your Policy	Your Partner's Policy
Employee contribution amount for family policy	_____	_____
Co-pays	_____	_____
Deductibles	_____	_____
Prescription costs	_____	_____
Yearly maximums	_____	_____
Lifetime maximum benefits	_____	_____

Learning About Additional Hospital Costs

If you will be going to a hospital or birth center, find out what out-of-pocket expenses you will be responsible for. In the hospital there are additional charges for:

- Telephone
- Television
- Private rooms

Call the billing department and ask about these costs and budget for them. If you will be giving birth in a birth center, find out if they have additional charges for these items and, if so, what they are. Add these costs to your parenthood budget.

Revising Your Pregnancy Budget

If you've had a baby shower, it's time to revise your list of things you need. Cross off items you've received and see what must-have items you're still missing. Head out to the store and pick up the essentials. You'll be getting gifts when the baby arrives, so only buy those things you'll need right away.

Check your budget against what you still need to buy and be sure to save some money for last-minute spending. Leave yourself a little flexibility. Remember that many of the items on your must-have list may not become essential for several months, so you have time to save for these expenses and shop for good deals. Once you're a parent you'll have a better idea of what will work best for both you and your baby. Something that looks great to you now may end up being impractical or difficult to use. Items that were must-haves for one child might not be needed at all for later children (for example, your first child might love being in a swing, but a subsequent child might hate it).

Return Policies

If you received duplicate shower gift items, you may need to return some things. The easiest way is to ask for the receipt from the gift giver. Many experienced moms will slip a gift receipt right in the box with your gift, so be sure to check before you dispose of any boxes. If you don't feel able to ask for a receipt, determine if the item is something on your registry. If it is, you should have no problem returning it for a store credit. If the item is not from your registry, try to figure out where it came from. Big-name baby care products and equipment can usually be returned at one of the major discount stores, such as Wal-Mart, for a store credit. Clothing can be harder to return. Keep in mind that you'll be doing a lot of laundry and it might be helpful to have duplicate outfits for the baby. If all else fails and you really don't want the item, can't figure out where it came from, and don't want to regift it, you can always donate it to charity and take a deduction on your tax return.

185
...

You can also sell items you don't want on eBay (www.ebay.com). If you do, specify that they are brand-new and unused. If the tags are still attached, note that in your listing as well. There are a variety of ways to list things on eBay, including an auction or a "Buy

It Now" listing where purchasers don't need to bid and can purchase immediately. It is helpful to post photos of items you are selling.

Your Lifestyle

What to Take When It's Time to Have the Baby

Get that bag packed. If you will be practicing any special method of childbirth, check with your instructor or check your pregnancy books to find out if there are special things you will need to bring. Be sure to pack:

- Nursing bras and nursing pads
- Socks and slippers
- Nursing nightgown
- Bathrobe
- Soft, loose clothing to wear home
- Your camera (and more film than you could possibly use or extra memory sticks, and the cord to recharge your camera or extra batteries)
- Phone numbers of family and friends to call after the birth
- A book or magazine to read during your postpartum stay
- Your glasses or contacts, if you wear them (if you have a C-section, you will be asked to remove your contacts)
- Toothbrush, toothpaste, deodorant, and shampoo if you want to use your own brands
- Contact lens supplies, if needed
- A hairbrush or comb and basic makeup (if you really think you will use it postpartum)
- An outfit for the baby to wear home
- Receiving blankets to use on the way home
- CDs to play while in labor
- A photo or other object to use as a focal point
- A snack for your labor coach

- Your own pillow if you want one from home
- Your own sanitary pads (hospital pads may not have wings or adhesives)
- Lip balm
- Your cord blood kit
- Your newborn testing packet
- Your health care directive
- Your health insurance card
- Your birth plan

Leave your cell phone at home, since cell phone use is not permitted in hospitals. If your partner brings his cell phone, make sure he turns it off while in the hospital. If he wants to make calls on it, he will need to leave the building to do so.

Subscribing to Parenting Magazines

Having a parenting magazine arrive in your mailbox each month with advice from experts, solutions to problems, tips from other parents, and information you may need can be a lifesaver. If you haven't received a subscription as a shower gift, consider subscribing to one of these magazines:

- *Parents*, www.Parents.com
- *Parenting*, www.Parenting.com
- *Child*, www.child.com

It's always a good idea to look at some issues at the library before subscribing. You may also have received special offers in the mail. Some of the magazines offer free gifts for subscribing. There may also be a regional parenting magazine for your area. Your local library should carry it if there is one, or you can check with the Parenting Publications of America (www.ParentingPublica tions.org). These magazines are often free and can be picked up at supermarkets, libraries, and day care centers and may also be available by a subscription through the mail.

Making Things Easier on Yourself

You might already be at that point when you're just waiting for the baby to finally come, too tired to do anything. Even if you're not, that day will soon come. And once you bring home the baby, you're going to be physically, mentally, and emotionally exhausted. Give yourself a break and take steps to make life a little easier now and in the coming months with these tips:

- Buy premoistened, disposable cleaning wipes for the bathroom, kitchen, mirrors, and furniture.
- Set up online banking so you can transfer money and pay bills without leaving the house.
- Buy stamps so you have plenty on hand for thank-you notes and paying bills.
- Buy scrapbooking material if you plan to work on a baby scrapbook.
- Stock up on toilet paper, tissues, plastic storage bags, paper plates and cups, and other products.
- Collect take-out menus and keep them near the phone.
- Withdraw some cash and keep it in a safe place so you don't need to run out to the ATM.
- Keep at least half a tank of gas in the car so you won't need to get it on the way to the hospital.
- Pay bills at least a week in advance so that you won't fall behind.
- Find out now how to turn the ringer off on your phone and the volume down on your answering machine. When you are home with the new baby, you may wish not to be disturbed.

Educating Yourself About Breastfeeding

The choice to breastfeed is a personal one. To help with this decision, educate yourself about breastfeeding and determine if it will be right for you and your baby. A good place to start is: www.Breast feedingBasics.org, which offers a free online course in breast-

Breastfeeding Books

The Nursing Mother's Companion by Kathleen Huggins (Harvard Common Press, 1999, $13.95).

The American Academy of Pediatrics New Mother's Guide to Breastfeeding (Bantam, 2002, $13.95).

The Breastfeeding Book by Martha and William Sears (Little, Brown and Company, 2000, $14.95).

The Ultimate Breastfeeding Book of Answers by Jack Newman (Prima Lifestyles, 2000, $19.95).

The Complete Book of Breastfeeding by Marvin S. Eiger and Sally Wendkos Olds (Workman, 1999, $10.95).

feeding. You can also obtain information at: www.lalecheleague.org and www.usbreastfeeding.org.

Talk with your health care provider about calorie/dietary requirements for nursing mothers and restrictions on alcohol, caffeine, and medications. If you are worried about your ability to breastfeed, discuss this as well. If you just aren't sure whether you are committed to breastfeeding, buy a few bottles and some formula in case you decide not to breastfeed. You may wish to breastfeed for a few months and then switch to bottles, so having some on hand will make the decision to switch easier.

Thinking About Home Safety

To get your home ready for your baby, take these basic safety precautions:

• The National Fire Protection Association (www.nfpa.org) recommends that you install a smoke alarm on each floor of your home and outside each bedroom. Mount them on ceilings or high on the walls and keep them away from windows or ducts. Test them once a month and replace batteries once a year. You should also have a carbon monoxide monitor installed in your home.

- Create a fire escape plan and rehearse it.
- Purchase outlet covers. Your baby won't be crawling for several months, so you can wait to install them until then.
- The Window Covering Safety Council (www.windowcover ings.com) recommends that you eliminate loops on miniblinds (they are a strangulation hazard). Never place a child's bed or crib next to miniblinds or place a chair or anything else a child can climb onto near a window. If you have blinds with cords, make sure they are tied down tightly or replace all miniblinds with roller shades or curtains.
- Make sure your changing table has a safety belt.
- Be sure there is a rug underneath your crib and changing table in case the baby should fall.
- Never place a night-light near your child's crib or bed.
- Make sure that any chests in your home do not have heavy, hinged, or locking lids.
- Remove space heaters from your child's room.

Writing Shower Thank-You Notes

If you had a baby shower or have already received gifts, get the thank-you notes done now and out of your hair before the baby comes. If you created labels on the computer, print them out and use them for the envelopes. Try to write one or two notes a day so that you aren't overwhelmed. Consult the log of gifts from your shower so you know whom to thank for what. Check off each gift as you write the note for it.

Finalizing the Baby's Room

Now's the time to let your nesting instinct take over. Get the nursery finished and enjoy putting everything in its place. Lay in a supply of diapers (buy newborn and size 1 so that you'll have some that will fit no matter what), baby wipes, and diaper rash cream.

If you'll be using formula, stock up on that. Remove all tags from clothing, bedding, and linens and wash the fabrics in gentle baby detergent (such as Dreft) so they are ready to use. However, if you don't know your baby's sex, leave the tags on the gender-specific items until the baby is born so that you can return them if necessary. If you will be breastfeeding, make sure you have enough nursing pads, a tube of lanolin (which will help with sore nipples), a nursing pillow, and a comfortable chair. Buy a head of cabbage and put it in the refrigerator. Putting the chilled leaves inside your bra will help with nipple and breast pain once your milk comes in. If you haven't bought a breast pump, get one now (see Chapter 7).

Make up the crib or bassinet and enjoy how cozy it looks. If you have any electronic toys for the baby or a monitor that uses batteries, buy extra batteries so you have them on hand. If you haven't already done so, buy a few different brands of pacifiers. Some babies prefer certain brands, since they are all shaped differently. If you have a mobile, secure it over the crib.

Set up your diaper changing area, with a changing pad, diapers, wipes, and a place to dispose of the diapers. If you live in a two-story home, set up diaper changing stations on both floors of the house so that you won't have to climb stairs to change diapers when you are first home from the hospital. Pack a diaper bag with a few diapers, wipes, and a changing pad so that if you need to take the baby out in the first few days, you will be packed and ready.

If you have a baby monitor, set it up and test it to be sure it works. Put away your breastfeeding or bottle-feeding supplies. Disinfect bottle-feeding supplies and breast pump parts and store in a sealed plastic bag so that if you need them, they are ready to go. Buy a box of maxi pads for use when you return home. Because postpartum bleeding is heavy, buy the best pads you can find with the most coverage and with wings.

Buying a Baby Memory Book

You'll want to record all of your baby's milestones and special moments from the very beginning because some of the most special memories are those that happen in the first few days at home. You won't want to have to run out to buy a book when you get home, so get one now.

Baby Memory Books

Goodnight Moon Baby Journal by Hurd Brown (Peaceable Kingdom Press, 2000, $12.95).

Oh Baby!: A Journal by Helene Tragos Stelian Stewart (Tabori & Chang, 2001, $18.95).

A Baby Book for You by Boston Museum of Fine Arts (Bulfinch, 1996, $17.95).

Baby's First Year Journal by A. Christine Harris (Chronicle Books, 1999, $19.95).

Baby's First Tattoo: A Memory Book for Modern Parents by Jim Mullen (Simon & Schuster, 2002, $12.95).

Month 9 Checklist

☐ Learn about your employer's policies on flextime and job sharing.
☐ Solidify your postpartum work schedule.
☐ Finalize your birth plan and ask questions about C-sections.
☐ Complete preadmission paperwork.
☐ Install your car seat and practice using it.
☐ Find out what you need to do to add the baby to your health insurance policy.
☐ Learn about additional hospital or birth center costs.
☐ Revise your pregnancy budget and buy necessities that you don't have yet.
☐ Return items you don't need.
☐ Pack your bag for when it's time to leave for the hospital.
☐ Subscribe to parenting magazines.

☐ Arrange your home and stock up on items so that things will be easy when you return home with the baby.
☐ Talk to your health care provider about breastfeeding.
☐ Do a safety check of your home.
☐ Write shower thank-you notes.
☐ Wash baby clothes, bedding, and linens.
☐ Stock up on diapers, wipes, formula, and nursing pads.
☐ Finalize the baby's room.
☐ Buy a baby memory book.

11

Labor, Delivery, and Postpartum Care

*M*aria was in labor and she and her husband had just arrived *at the hospital. Her OB (who practiced alone) was doing a C-section with another patient and would not be able to see her anytime soon. Unfortunately, Maria's labor was progressing very rapidly. Maria took an instant dislike to the dotor on call. He knew nothing about what she wanted and seemed not to care. Finally, she told him she did not want him to deliver her baby. Another doctor was quickly brought in and delivered Maria's baby. Though this kind of turmoil was upsetting, Maria was happy with her decision and felt that her birth experience had*

The day your baby arrives is probably one of the most important days in your life. It will also be a very busy day with a lot happening and little time to think. Thinking now about the decisions and situations you may face will help you focus on the important moment—the birth of your baby.

been a good one because she was able to work with a doctor who listened to what she wanted and who was willing to work with her.

Your Rights

Dealing with Admissions

When it's time to go to the hospital or birth center, bring your health insurance card. You will also need to know your social security number. If you preregistered, there should be very little paperwork to take care of, other than verifying who you are. If you did not preregister, you will be asked to sign forms permitting the facility to treat you and submit your bills to your insurance company. (See Chapter 10 for more information on admissions paperwork.)

When you are in labor you should go directly to the maternity ward or emergency room (check with your facility to find out where you should enter). Don't wait in a line in admissions. You're in labor and you don't have time to sit in a waiting room. The staff will expedite your admissions paperwork.

Your Rights While in Labor

You are not at the mercy of the hospital or birth center when you are in labor. It may feel like you have very little control over what happens, but in fact you have complete control over your body and have the right to ask questions and make decisions about treatment.

You should have given a copy of your birth plan to your health care provider during your pregnancy. Bring a copy with you and give it to him or her again if he or she doesn't seem to remember, but understand that a birth plan is just an advance plan for how you want things to go. You can change your mind as things progress.

You can refuse any treatment that is not lifesaving. In some states, laws require you to accept treatment that will protect your baby's life, such as a C-section, if medically necessary. Other than lifesaving treatment, you can say no to anything. If you don't want to lie on your back, you don't have to. If you want to walk around, you can insist that you be permitted to. You can choose not to accept monitoring devices (internal or external probes to track the baby's heartbeat), but you have to understand the risks involved in not accepting this kind of treatment.

You have the right to choose the position you deliver in, but you must be aware that your health care provider may agree to work with you only in certain positions (this should have come up when you shared your birth plan with him or her during pregnancy). Your health care provider and the nurses caring for you are more experienced at this than you are and may be able to tell you what position might be more comfortable or more successful for you. You can ask for a second opinion at any time in the labor process; however, during delivery there is usually no time for a second opinion. If during labor you ask for a second opinion and agree with what the second provider has said, you can switch providers.

If this is your first baby, the entire labor and delivery experience is going to be a new experience for you, no matter how well prepared you are. Don't be afraid to raise concerns, ask questions, and talk to the people who are providing care for you. If something doesn't seem right, speak up. If you're scared, tell them. If you're in pain, tell them. If you feel you can't go on, tell them. The staff is there to help you, not to work against you, and you must use this resource to fill your needs.

Maintaining Privacy

Much ado is made about maintaining the privacy of medical records, but hospitals are often places where personal privacy is hard to come by. Your right to privacy was discussed in Chapter 2.

Here are some things you can do to retain at least an illusion of privacy:

- Wear a robe, or a second hospital gown backward, so that you are completely covered.
- Close the curtain or door to your area.
- Ask that students or interns not participate in your care.
- Cover yourself with a sheet if you feel exposed.
- Focus on your labor coach or your focal point and block out the staff in the room.
- Ask that lights be dimmed in between exams.
- Use the bathroom alone when possible and close the door unless you need assistance.
- Ask to be placed on the list for a private postpartum room as soon as you arrive.
- If you have a roommate in your postpartum room, ask that exams be done in a separate exam room.

Baby Identification Tags

All hospitals use identification tags to identify the babies. After your baby is born, the hospital should place a bracelet on his or her wrist and ankle, and a matching tag on your wrist. Ask to see the identifying tags on all the bracelets (or have your partner check them) to verify accuracy. When the baby is brought to you, the tags should be checked against yours every single time. If the hospital issues bracelets to fathers, his should be checked if he comes into the nursery to get the baby.

Birth Certificates

Your hospital or birth center will provide you with the paperwork to apply for a birth certificate after your baby is born. If you do not receive this application, let a nurse know. If you get no response, call the facility's patient advocate and ask for assistance.

If for some reason you are not able to get the form while in the hospital or birth center, contact your health care provider's office.

Some parents don't feel ready to make a decision about the baby's name right after the birth. Don't panic if this happens to you. Sometimes it just takes time to find the right name. You can leave the birth certificate blank and select a first name later or you can choose one and change it later. To change a name on a birth certificate, contact your local office of the department of vital statistics (check the white government pages in your phone book, or call the town in which the certificate was issued for information about whom to contact). If you make a name change in the first few weeks after the birth, all you need to do is complete a new form requesting the change and it will be processed and a new birth certificate issued. Should you want to change the child's name later in life, you will need a court order.

Baby Photos in the Hospital

Almost all hospitals now have a photographer who comes into the room and takes photographs of newborns. The photos are then offered to you in a package to purchase. Though many parents are happy to have this service available to them, others are not interested. You have the right to request that your baby not be photographed, and if you do allow photographs to be taken, you don't have to buy them. If you don't want the photograph taken, let the nursery know this as soon as possible after the birth. You can also ask at what time the photos are taken each day and arrange to have your baby in your room at that time. If you say nothing, they will take the photo.

199

Many hospitals also provide a service in which your baby's photo and information can be posted on a special Web page. These Web pages can be accessed only by using a password, which you will receive. This is an optional service and you can decline. Again, just notify the nursery as soon as possible that you don't want your baby listed. This service can be a great time-saver, though, so you don't have to go home and e-mail details to everyone. You or the other parent can send everyone a link to the page, and all the information will be available there once they enter the password you provide.

Acknowledgment and Registry of Paternity for Unmarried Parents

Lots of parents have children together without marrying. If you and your partner are not married, the hospital or birth facility should not treat you any differently. If your child will take his father's last name, you will need to let the facility know this, otherwise he will be referred to using your last name.

If you and the other parent are a heterosexual couple, register the birth with the state putative father registry. (See Chapter 1 for more information.) The baby's father is then listed on the birth certificate and is the legal parent. Married couples do not need to do this because the husband is legally the father of any child his wife gives birth to.

If you and the other parent have a difficult relationship but still agree he is the father, it is important to register paternity so that you will have access to child support. If it is unclear who the baby's father is, you will need to go to your state's family court and have a paternity case brought so that DNA can be compared to determine the biological father. If you are unsure who the father is, you can list someone on the birth certificate, but this often will complicate things if you do go to court and someone else is the actual father. If you don't know, it's best to leave it blank. If you do know, but he doesn't know and you don't want him to know, you can also leave it blank.

Documenting a Home Birth

If you're one of the 27,000 U.S. parents each year who chooses a home birth, make sure that you take the necessary steps to document the birth so that a birth certificate can be issued. If a mid-

wife assists your baby's birth, she may be able to issue a birth certificate. Ask this question when you are planning your baby's birth.

If you do not use a professional birth attendant or your midwife
cannot issue a birth certificate, contact your state department of
vital records to determine what you should do. In most states you
will need to complete a form and have it notarized (you can do so
at your bank). You may also be able to have the first physician that
examines your baby submit a form.

No matter how it is documented, it is important that a home
birth is reported quickly. Each state has different time periods, so
it's important that you check and find out what your state's requirements are. Your child will need a birth certificate in order to get a
social security number, passport, or driver's license.

Refusing Treatment for Your Baby

You are in charge of making health care decisions for your baby.
As your child's parent, you can refuse treatment that is not lifesaving. You are required to comply with your state's newborn testing laws (unless you can prove an exception), but other than that,
you can decide the type of treatment and care your baby will
receive. This includes:

- Bottle-feeding
- Circumcision
- Surgery
- Tests (such as X-rays or CT scans)
- Medications
- Pacifier use
- Feeding schedule

Dealing with Lactation Consultants

If you give birth in a hospital and are breastfeeding, you will probably receive a visit from a lactation consultant while you are there.
Your pediatrician may also ask you to set up an appointment with

a lactation consultant on staff in the office. Meeting with a lactation consultant can be a huge relief if you are having problems breastfeeding. Your lactation consultant can help you with latching on, learning when the baby has had enough, keeping the baby awake while feeding, and more.

For some women, though, a visit from a lactation consultant is embarrassing. You're expected to feed your baby then and there in front of a stranger. If you're not having any problems nursing, nothing says you have to accept any help or nurse on command. However, if you're having any difficulties, it's best to push embarrassment or shyness aside and get help. Lactation consultants have seen hundreds of breasts, and they aren't going to be shocked or surprised by yours. It's also important to know that lactation specialists have good solutions to problems you might think are unsolvable, so it is always a good idea to ask if you have any difficulties. To find out where to get information about breastfeeding, see Chapter 10.

Beginning Maternity/Paternity/Parenting Leave

If you haven't already made arrangements for maternity, disability, or paternity leave, address this within the first day or two after the birth. Contact your human resources department and let them know that you have given birth and will be taking a leave. If there are any remaining documents to be signed or completed, ask to have them e-mailed, faxed, or mailed to you. Also make sure that any paychecks or payments that will be issued to you will be sent to your home or directly deposited into your bank account.

Getting Information After the Birth

When you give birth in a hospital or birth center, there are a wide variety of resources available to you. Many facilities have a special baby care channel on the television or videos that you can watch. All facilities have lactation specialists on staff who can assist you with breastfeeding. Most facilities offer classes every day for new mothers about breastfeeding and baby care. Ask a staff member if there are any available and how to take part in them. Additionally, you may also be given brochures and printouts with information that will help you through the first few weeks of parenting and caring for your postbirth body. Remember that the staff is there not just to provide medical care but also to educate, so ask questions and seek help whenever you need to.

After you go home you may find that you have questions or concerns. Your first step should be to call your health care provider or your baby's pediatrician. If you can't get the help you need over the phone, make an appointment. Many hospitals provide maternity patients with a phone number for the maternity ward so that they can call there with any questions in the first few weeks. Keep this phone number on a bulletin board or close to the phone so that you can find it if you need it.

Meals

Hospital food is notorious for being bad, but if you are on a restricted diet, it is important that you eat what you are given. If you are not on a restricted diet, you don't have to eat their food if you don't want to. Some hospitals have alternative menus that allow you to order from the cafeteria that is open to the public. Additionally, visitors can bring you any food you would like. If you won't be eating the hospital meals, it is a good idea to let the staff know, so that a meal is not sent to your room.

Taking Charge of Your Baby's Care

If this is your first child, being a parent is a whole new experience for you. It's easy to feel as though the professionals around you know what's best for your child, but in reality, you are the one who knows (yes, even now!) your child best. It can be hard to step up and take control of the situation, particularly if your baby is having any kind of health problem, but it is essential that you make it known to all the health care providers that you are in control of your child's treatment and that you must have complete information and explanations. It can be hard to get answers in a hospital, when doctors are moving around and are difficult to find. But you must make it clear that you need answers and that you want to make informed decisions. Refuse to sign consent forms without complete information. If you want to talk to a doctor, ask that he or she be paged. Call your pediatrician's office and ask who is on call at the hospital and ask that he or she come to see you. Ask questions of the nursery staff, even if you have to walk (or go in a wheelchair) down there. You have the right to a second opinion, and you may call in any specialist you want.

Visitors

Most facilities have loose visiting hours for fathers (which includes unmarried heterosexual partners but may not include same-sex partners—check on this in advance). Regular visiting hours don't usually apply, and it's rare that anyone will try to enforce them. Many fathers are able to spend the night in the mother's room, and some rooms have chairs that fold out into a cot for this purpose. Even if this is not the case, if you want your partner to stay, most hospitals will accommodate him. If you do plan on having your partner stay overnight, you can inquire about the rules in advance. If it is against the rules, you can probably still get away with it if you are discrete and don't make a fuss about it. It's unlikely that anyone is going to ask him to leave if he is quietly snoozing in a chair in the corner. But if he's marching up and down the halls in the middle of the night causing a ruckus, you will have a problem. Note also that the showers on the maternity ward are for the patients only.

Maternity wards are often fairly flexible about other guests and may not make your guests strictly adhere to the visiting hours. Children are allowed to visit their mothers and siblings in the maternity ward, even though they may not be permitted in the rest of the hospital. If you have other children, you may wish to set up a special time for them to meet their new sibling and spend some time with you together as a family, without any other visitors around.

It is up to you and your partner to control the number and length of visits. If you want time to rest, have your partner let people know this by phone. If you welcome guests, have him convey this. If you become tired while guests are there, speak up and let them know. If you have a roommate, you will want to be considerate of her needs as well. Many hospitals have family rooms or seating areas where you and your guests can go to talk.

Checking Out

When it's time to leave the hospital, make sure you pack all of your belongings as well as any sample items you've been given. If you have expressed and stored milk, ask for a cooler bag in which to take it home. Alert the nursing staff that you're ready to go. They may ask you to sign some papers indicating that you were instructed on how to care for yourself and the baby. You will also need to sign an acknowledgment that you are being discharged. Once the discharge paperwork has been completed, get yourself dressed and ready first. Dress the baby last. Have your partner pack up everything in the room and make sure he checks the bathroom, closet, and drawers (if there are any). If you don't want to take the flowers home that you have received, you can ask the nursing staff to give them to other patients who may not have any.

Your partner may be sent to get the car, and in most hospitals you and the baby will be taken to the exit in a wheelchair. Do not remove your identifying bracelets until you are home.

When you check out, make sure you bring:

- All of your belongings that you brought into the hospital
- Flowers, cards, and gifts
- Free samples from the nursery
- Postpartum instructions from your health care provider
- Information provided by your pediatrician in the hospital (such as care instructions or baby care guides)

- Prescriptions
- Birth certificate paperwork, if you have not completed it
- Copies of your baby's footprints (if any are provided) and identifying card from the nursery

Leaving the Hospital Without Your Baby

Should your baby need to stay in the hospital longer than you do, don't panic. The most important thing is that she gets the care needed. It can be heartbreaking to have to leave the hospital without your baby in your arms as you had planned, but many hospitals can bend the rules for you a little for a few days. If there is an empty bed, they may let you sleep there (unofficially) so that you can be close to the baby. There may also be cots near the nursery available for parents to crash on. If your baby will have to stay, ask the nursery and maternity ward staff about policies. Keep asking different people until you get an answer you like. If no one will accommodate you, contact the patient advocate and explain your problem.

If you do end up leaving without your baby, focus on getting rest, eating, and staying calm. Talk with the hospital staff and your pediatrician about expressing milk during this period. Of course you will want to spend a lot of time visiting and caring for your baby, but you must recognize that the staff is very well trained and will provide proper care and that it is OK for you to go home and rest.

Your Finances

Handling Unforeseen Expenses in the Hospital

Despite your best plans, you may have unforeseen expenses from the birth. This might include medical care that is not covered by your insurance or the additional cost of a private room. If your costs are large, someone from the billing department might contact you before you leave to talk about how you will pay for the expenses. Most hospitals are willing to work out payment plans. They can't stop you from leaving even if you have no way to pay for the costs, but they can use a collection agency or service to attempt to get you to pay in the months after the birth. If you have unexpected expenses, your best plan is to first have the costs resubmitted to your insurance. If you thought something was covered, there may have been an error. You can appeal any denial of coverage (talk to the patient advocate at the hospital for help with this). If there was no mistake, then working out a payment plan is your best option for dealing with the cost.

If there has been a sudden change in your financial circumstances and you no longer have health insurance, ask to speak to the hospital social worker. You or your child may be eligible for low- or no-cost health insurance through a state government program.

Your Lifestyle

Staying Comfortable
Once you've been moved to your room in the hospital, there are a number of things you can do to make it feel more comfortable.

- Have your partner rearrange the visitors' chairs into a more welcoming arrangement.
- Hang up cards people bring you on a bulletin board (if there is one) or display them on your nightstand or windowsill.
- Have your partner fill up your water pitcher with ice and a little water. The ice will melt and create a constant supply of cold water.
- Ask your partner to put your bag close to your bed so you can reach it.
- Place things you will be using frequently (a comb, a book, or glasses) next to you on a nightstand.

- Ask your partner to take your meal trays into the hall when you are done with them so they do not clutter the room.
- Find out if the hospital has snacks available for mothers and have your partner bring a supply into your room so they are there if you want them.
- Put on your own clothing or sleepwear.
- Wash your hands frequently and ask visitors to do the same. Hospitals are filled with germs and you don't want you or your baby to catch anything.
- Wear slippers or shoes when walking on cold hospital floors.
- Turn off lights in the room and close the door or curtain when you want to sleep.

Dealing with Nerves

Once you've had your baby, you might feel comfortable and happy in your new role as a mom, or you might feel suddenly terrified that you are responsible for this new little person. It's OK to be nervous. Reassure yourself that mothering really is a natural skill. If you need help, ask the nursing staff. Talk to your friends and relatives and ask for advice and reassurance. Take some quick peeks in your baby care books or at the hospital baby care TV channel if you need expert advice.

Labor, Delivery, and Postpartum Care Checklist

☐ Make sure you and your baby wear matching bracelets.

☐ Apply for birth certificate.

☐ Take home expressed milk and free samples.

☐ Choose whether or not to purchase hospital baby photos.

☐ Find out if the hospital has a website where your baby's photo and information can be displayed, and decide if you want to participate.

☐ Complete any paperwork or notifications needed for maternity leave.

☐ Complete discharge paperwork.

12

Parenthood

*B*aby Lisa goes to day care while Chrissie and Tyler are at work. One day Chrissie was out of town and Tyler was supposed to pick Lisa up after work. His boss called him into his office at 5:00 and wanted him to completely revamp a project they had been working on. The day care closes at 5:30 and Tyler was frantic. He excused himself from the meeting and quickly called his sister Stephanie and asked her to go pick Lisa up. When Stephanie got there, the day care center refused to let her take Lisa because she was not authorized to do so. The center tried to call Tyler on his cell phone at the office, but he could not be reached. When he got out of the meeting at 7:00, he had several

Congratulations on becoming a parent! You've made it through the challenges and drama of pregnancy and delivery, and now you can enjoy life with your new addition. Just as with pregnancy, there are lots of things to think about and manage as you raise your baby, and this section is designed to help guide you through decisions and steps you need to take.

messages on his phone and raced to pick up Lisa. The day care director had to stay late to care for Lisa and she handed Tyler a bill that charged him in fifteen-minute increments for the overtime. After this, Chrissie and Tyler completed an authorization form allowing Stephanie or Chrissie's mom to pick up Lisa.

Your Rights

Finalization of Wills
Once you've settled in at home with the baby, you must be sure to finalize and sign a new will that lists your child as a beneficiary and names a guardian for him or her. If you haven't already discussed this with an attorney, make an appointment and get a will drawn up. See Chapter 6 for more information.

Sending in Life Insurance Beneficiary Changes
After you're settled in at home, you should also send in life insurance beneficiary change forms now so that your child is listed as the primary or alternate beneficiary.

Traveling with Your Baby
If you will be traveling out of the country with your child, he or she will need a passport. You can obtain the forms online and have them processed at the post office. You will need a small photo of your child that meets passport regulations. For more information about passports, go to: http://travel.state.gov/passport.

If you are traveling by air, you are not required to purchase a separate seat for your child until he or she is two years old. However this means you will have to hold the baby on your lap the entire flight. If you want to be able to place him or her in a car seat, purchase an extra seat. The Federal Aviation Administration recommends that all children be secured in approved safety seats until they reach forty pounds. You may be able to get a discount of 50 percent for your baby, so be sure to ask.

State-Required Immunizations

Each state has immunizations that are required before children enter school. Most states have laws that allow an exception to the requirements for religious reasons. The American Academy of Pediatrics has a list of recommended immunizations online at: www.immunize.org/catg.d/when1.pdf. There are currently seventeen immunizations recommended between birth and age two. Though it's not fun to see your child get an immunization, it is an important way to safeguard his or her health. Some parents have concerns about the safety of immunizations and possible side effects. The American Academy of Pediatrics recommends that most children be immunized. If you have any concerns or questions, discuss them with your pediatrician.

Planning for Medical Care for Your Child in Your Absence

If you will be leaving your baby with a relative, make plans to ensure that your baby will be able to receive medical care when you're not available. Although hospitals and pediatricians will provide care if a child's life or limb is in danger, they cannot provide nonemergency care without parental consent. To avoid problems, give your child's caregiver a written authorization to obtain care for your baby. Here is an example:

211

I, Melinda Rogers, authorize Sally Rogers to obtain any and all emergency and nonemergency medical care for my daughter, Alexis Rogers.

_____   _____
name   date

It is important to note that doctors will do everything they can to get authorization to treat your child and will usually accept a verbal authorization over the phone. Your child's pediatrician may also have a policy that he or she will treat your child in the office, no matter who brings him or her in. To be safe, though, write up an authorization and keep it in the diaper bag.

Second Opinions and Changing Providers

As your baby grows, you'll be spending a lot of time at your pediatrician's office, so it's important to be comfortable with your child's health care provider. If you ever have a situation where you feel you aren't getting the answers you need, you have the right to seek a second opinion. Sometimes parents can be dissatisfied with the nurse practitioner or physician assistant whom they see for sick visits, so be sure to ask to see the doctor if you are not satisfied with the level of care you are receiving.

If you do decide you want a second opinion, call your insurance company to make sure one is covered. If you want to take your child to a specialist, you may be required to have your child's pediatrician write a referral. If you would like to see another pediatrician, get recommendations from family and friends. Call the new doctor's office and explain you would like a second opinion.

You can also decide to change pediatricians permanently if you find one you are more comfortable with. Determine that this new doctor is accepting new patients, and then contact your insurance company and find out what paperwork you need to complete to make the change.

Breastfeeding

If you're breastfeeding and working, you probably will need to pump while at the office. There is a huge variation in how helpful employers can be when it comes to breastfeeding mothers. Some companies designate separate rooms and give employees extra breaks for pumping. Others make no accommodation at all. Before you return to work, have a conversation with your human resources contact about what accommodations can be made for you. Connecticut, Hawaii, Illinois, and Minnesota require employers to accommodate breastfeeding mothers.

Many women are worried about how breastfeeding at work will impact their jobs. It is illegal for an employer to discriminate against you because you are breastfeeding. This means that you cannot be fired, demoted, or treated differently because you are breastfeeding. If you present pumping as something that won't interfere with your job, your employer is more likely to agree. Some inexperienced employers envision pumping taking up hours. If you present a reasonable pumping schedule, most employers won't have a problem with it. You don't need to tell your employer you are breastfeeding, unless you want him or her to make special accommodations for you to pump.

If a separate room is not specifically designated for pumping and you feel you need one, ask if there is an office, break room, conference room, or other space with a door you can use, and explain why most bathrooms are not suitable. Hang a sign on the door that says "Privacy please" or "Do not disturb," if you wish. Keep your expressed milk in the company refrigerator or in a cooler bag with ice. Begin pumping at home two weeks before you will return to work and try to set up an abbreviated work schedule your first week back. For information about breastfeeding and working, contact The National Women's Health Information Center at: www.4woman.gov, or call 800-994-9662. The site offers free publications, such as:

- *Breastfeeding: Returning to Work*: www.breastfeeding basics.org/pi/pi-165.pdf
- *Using a Breast Pump*: www.mayoclinic.com/invoke.cfm ?id=PR00002
- *Breastfeeding Basics: Returning to Work or School*: www .nncc.org/Nutrition/bf5.return.html

Books About Nursing and Working
Nursing Mother, Working Mother: The Essential Guide for Breastfeeding and Staying Close to Your Baby After You Return to Work by Gale Pryor (Harvard Common Press, 1997, $11.95).

Breastfeeding Laws
About half of all states have laws that make it clear that breast-feeding is not indecent or prohibited in public. Even in states where specific laws have not been enacted, you have the right to feed your baby whenever and wherever you wish. There is also a federal law that makes it clear women have the right to breastfeed anywhere, anytime on federal property.

California, Idaho, Iowa, and Oregon have laws that exempt breastfeeding mothers from jury duty. If you are called for jury duty and your state does not have a breastfeeding exemption, you might qualify for a child care provider exemption (if you provide full-time care for your child) or for a hardship exemption. It can also be help-ful to ask your pediatrician to send a letter explaining that dis-rupting breastfeeding is detrimental to both you and your baby.

Read about your state's breastfeeding laws online at: www.la lecheleague.org/Law/summary.html.

Grandparents' Rights

If you have a difficult relationship with your parents, or with your child's other grandparents, the issue of grandparents' rights is one to be concerned with. If you believe that your child's grandparents cannot adequately care for him or her or feel they are a threat to your child, you are wise to limit visits, but you may wish to con-sider allowing the grandparents to come to your home to spend time with the baby while you are there. Some parents are reluctant to allow grandparents to spend time with their child because of long-standing bad feelings, misunderstandings, or family rifts. A grandchild can often help heal these rifts, so this may be a good time to consider whether the relationship can be saved.

The Supreme Court has weighed in on grandparents' rights in the 2000 case of *Troxel v. Granville*. That decision limited grandparents' rights and held that parents can decide what kind of relationship the child will have with the grandparents. All states have some type of grandparent visitation law that allows grandparents to ask the court to formally give them time with their grandchildren. Most states allow grandparents to seek this kind of order only if the child's parents are divorced or if one is deceased. Other states will grant visitation whenever it is in the best interest of the child, but this can be a difficult standard for grandparents to meet.

If you are certain you don't want your child's grandparents to be part of your child's life, then it makes sense to keep them out from the beginning. Once they begin to establish a relationship with the child, their role in the child's life becomes more important. Courts are more willing to hear these types of cases when a grandparent has a long-standing role in a child's life and is then suddenly cut off. If you do not want your child's grandparents in his or her life, be sure that this wish is expressed in the guardianship section of your will (see Chapter 5).

If you find yourself in the middle of a grandparent visitation case, try to reach a settlement. Mediation can be particularly helpful in resolving these kinds of disputes. There are often a myriad of other issues that are involved in the case, particularly past events between parent and grandparent, and these kinds of things can be worked out more easily in mediation than in court.

Missing Children

No one wants to even imagine if their own child were missing, but it is important to take the time now to understand what you should do if this ever should happen to you. The Center for Missing and Exploited Children recommends that you:

- First search your house carefully to make sure the child has not moved or hidden.
- Immediately call local law enforcement if you cannot find your child.
- Provide your child's name, date of birth, weight, height, and other identifiers. It can also help to know what your child was wearing. It is useful to always have a current photo or video of your child.
- Request of your local authorities that your child's name and information be immediately entered into the National Crime Information Center (NCIC) Missing Person File.
- Call the National Center for Missing and Exploited Children at: 800-THE-LOST (800-843-5678) for more assistance.

If your child is missing in a store, immediately notify an employee and ask for a Code Adam (you can also just shout out "Code Adam"). This means they will seal all exits to prevent someone from leaving with your child. If you believe your child has been abducted and have any information about the vehicle, ask local law enforcement to put out an Amber Alert. This will post information about the abductor and his or her vehicle on highway signs across the state.

If you are concerned about possible abduction by a family member, consider applying for a passport for your child (you can do so at your local post office). Only one passport can be issued per child. Put it in a safe or safety deposit box. This will prevent anyone from removing your child from the country. Notify your day care provider that your child is not to be released under any circumstances to anyone other than you, and seek the assistance of an attorney.

Megan's Law

Megan's Law requires sex offenders to register their residences and makes this information available to the public. To find out about sex offenders in your area, visit the website for the National Center for Missing and Exploited Children at: www.missingkids.org, and click on "Sex-Offenders/Megan's Law." This will tell you if there is a sex offender in your area, but you can't force him or her to move (although free speech supports parents talking to each other and notifying other members in the community of the presence of a sex offender).

Child Abuse

If you ever suspect that anyone has harmed your child in any way, it is essential that you report it immediately to the local police or to your state department for children and families or social services. There will be a hotline number listed in the white government pages of your phone book that you can call, or you can just call 911.

If you suspect abuse but cannot prove it, keep your child away from the person you suspect. Some parents install hidden cameras in their homes to check up on nannies or sitters. Counter Spy Shops reports a 25 percent increase in sales of these items in the past ten years. It is legal in all states to use a hidden camera to tape a sitter or nanny in your home.

Your Finances

Even though your child is just a newborn, you have a lot of financial issues to address. In 2002 the U.S. Department of Agriculture estimated that families earning $65,800 a year or more spend $249,180 to raise a child from birth through age seventeen. Raising a child is not cheap by any means, so getting a handle on your finances now will help you in the long run.

217
. . .

Obtaining a Social Security Number

Your baby is going to need a social security number in order to have a bank account or to be included on your tax return. Some hospitals will provide you with the paperwork to apply for a social security number. You can also obtain the necessary form online at: www.ssa.gov/online/ss-5.html, or by visiting your local Social Security Administration office (check the government pages in your phone book for the location or find it online at: www.ssa.gov). Once you complete the form, you can either take it in person or mail it to the Social Security Administration office nearest you with your child's birth certificate. Many parents feel more comfortable taking the form there in person than sending it through the mail, since you must include your baby's birth certificate. If you choose to mail it, purchase a certified copy of the birth certificate from the town or city where it is filed and send that instead of the original. The card will be issued to you through the mail in about two weeks and the certificate will be returned. Once you receive the card, keep it in a safe place.

Adjusting Your Payroll Withholding for Dependents

Once your baby is born, you can adjust your payroll to reflect your new status as a parent. When you add dependents to your tax withholdings, less money is taken out of each paycheck. Some people prefer not to list all their dependents, have more taken out, and then get a refund each year. Others prefer to list all dependents, have very little withheld, and invest the money, so that if they end up owing the government taxes they will at least have earned interest on that money. You are not required to adjust your withholding when you add a child to your family, but if in the past you regularly got refunds, reducing your withholding will mean more cash in your pocket now. To change your withholding, contact your human resources department.

Tax Exemptions for New Babies

Your child is a dependent and thus you get to claim him or her as an exemption on your taxes. The exemption is deducted from your income before taxes are calculated. The amount of the exemption is adjusted each year for inflation. At the time this book was published, the exemption was $3,100 per child. Contact your tax preparer for current amounts. When you file your taxes for the calendar year the baby is born in, you can take a dependency exemption for your baby, as long as he or she lives with you and you provide at least half of his or her support. It doesn't matter when in the year your baby is born—anywhere from January 1 to December 31. As long as it is in that calendar year, you can claim a dependency exemption. If you are a single parent, file as the single head of household when you file your taxes. You can also claim the child care credit if your child goes to day care (see Chapter 8).

Bank Accounts

It is a good idea to set up a bank account for your baby. This gives you a place to deposit cash or checks you receive as gifts after the birth and a place to sock away monetary birthday and holiday gifts each year as well. The most common type of bank account used is the Uniform Gift to Minors Act (UGMA) account. This type of account is set up in the child's name with a parent as the custodian of the account. The parent has complete control over the account until the child is age eighteen or twenty-one (depending on your state's laws). You may also choose to open a Uniform Transfers to Minors Act (UTMA) account, which allows the parent to retain control of the account for a longer period of time, often until the child finishes college. All accounts will be registered under the child's social security number. You may be able to avoid fees and make depositing and transferring funds more convenient if you open your child's account with the bank in which you have your other accounts. Ask if the bank has any promotions for accounts for babies, such as a free small beginning deposit in the account. Be sure to open an account that will earn interest, no matter how low the rate. Keep a separate ledger for the account, and balance it as you would your own savings account. The first $750 deposited per year until your child is age fourteen is tax free. Keep your child's bank account statements in a separate file.

Investments

Investments can be handled as UGMA or UTMA accounts as well. You may wish to set up an investment account for your child if you plan on making regular deposits, because you will earn more interest than if you just leave the money in a savings account. You can also encourage family members to contribute to the investment account (this is something that will appeal to grandparents who are at a point in their lives when they realize how much money really is needed to retire).

Be aware, though, that as the law is today, money your child has in an investment account will be counted against him or her when applying for college financial aid. Some parents prefer to set up an account in their own names but set it aside in their minds as belonging to their child. Keep a separate file for your child's investment account and be sure to include regular savings in your parenthood budget.

Savings Bonds

You may receive some savings bonds as gifts for your child. Standard U.S. EE savings bonds are purchased at half of the face value. The full face value of the bond is reached twenty years after the date of issue. Once it reaches maturity it continues to earn interest until final maturity, which is thirty years after the purchase date. You can cash in your child's bond, even though it is in his or her name. Most banks are able to cash in bonds.

Use this online calculator to determine value of savings bonds: www.publicdebt.treas.gov/sav/savcalc.htm.

Savings bonds can be purchased online or in person. The bonds are then mailed to the recipient. If someone tells you they bought your child a bond and you don't receive it within fifteen days, contact the place of purchase. If the bond has not been cashed, it can be replaced.

For more information about U.S. savings bonds, go to: www.publicdebt.treas.gov/sav/sav.htm.

Developing a Long-Term Financial Plan for Your Child

It is not too soon to begin formulating a long-term financial plan for your child. The sooner you invest money for your child, the more years it has to grow and increase. Before you take any major steps (other than setting up a bank account), it is a good idea to talk to your financial planner so that you can devise a financial strategy that fits your income, goals, and plans. There are a lot of options available, but you must completely understand the consequences before jumping in. You may wish to set up a college savings plan (see below) or invest a certain amount each year into your child's bank or investment account. Anything you can invest now will have a longer time to grow and earn interest for your child's future. Kevin McKinley, author of *Make Your Kid a Millionaire* (Fireside, 2002, $13.00), says that if parents invest just forty-one cents per day from the day their child is born, that child will be a millionaire by age sixty-five. How and where you invest your money is key, so talk to your financial advisor about the best way to invest in your child's future.

College Savings Plans

Although your child is just a baby, it's not too soon to begin thinking about college. College costs grow 5 percent each year, so by the time your child is ready for college, the expense will be much greater than it is today. There are two main types of college savings plans available.

529 Plans

There are two types of 529 plans: prepaid plans and savings programs, which you add to gradually. Prepaid plans let you pay for your child's college tuition at today's prices. This can be attractive but only guarantees tuition at an in-state public school. If your child goes out-of-state or to a private college, you will be given the amount equivalent to in-state public tuition.

Both 529 investment plans are created by states (although the law now allows individual schools to offer plans) and offer a way to save money for college tax free. Money placed in the account is not taxed (in many states), and interest earned on money in the account is tax exempt. The funds must be used to pay for college expenses (including tuition, room and board, books, etc.). You can set up a 529 account at any point in your child's life, and the sooner you start, the more you can accumulate before college. You can open an account with a very small initial deposit, such as $25 in some cases. If you sign up for one right away, you can ask people to give gifts directly to the plan. Many people like to give a gift knowing they are directly impacting the child's future education.

These plans allow you to sign up for automatic transfers from your bank account into the plan, so you can create a monthly contribution plan. There are no income restrictions and the caps on amounts are very high. (In Nebraska, for example, you can contribute as much as $200,000.)

There is a 10 percent penalty on withdrawals that are not for educational expenses, so if your child doesn't go to college, or if you take out the money before then, you will have to pay the penalty (but the money *can* be transferred to another person in the family, so if you have another child who will be going to college, the money can be used for him or her). For these reasons it is a good idea to talk with a financial planner to determine how you should best save for college. Read about 529 plans at: www.saving forcollege.com/529_plans/state_pages/index.php. It's important to note that you are not required to use your state's plan and can choose from among all available plans. And most plans do not require that you use the money at a school within the plan's state—your child can go to college anywhere and use these funds. The plan chooses how the money is invested, so it's important you choose a plan that uses a strategy you agree with.

You may also wish to set up an account with Upromise (www .Upromise.com). You register your credit cards and grocery cards, and when you purchase qualifying products, money is paid into your Upromise account, which can then be transferred directly to your child's 529 plan.

Coverdell Education Savings

Coverdell Education Savings was once known as education IRAs. With this type of plan you control how the money is invested, and some parents prefer to have this type of control. You can contribute up to $2,000 per child per year tax free to this account and can only do so if your joint income is under $190,000 ($95,000 on an individual return). The money must be used before the child turns thirty years old. This money counts as your child's asset when applying for financial aid. These plans don't allow you to save as much as a 529 plan and require you to be actively involved in choosing an investment strategy.

Cashing Checks in Your Baby's Name

It is likely that you will receive some checks as gifts from relatives made out in your baby's name. You're probably not going to run out to the bank and open an account for your child in the first month when you're still trying to get sleep and pull your life together, so instead, simply write on the back "Pay to the order of" and then write your name. Underneath this, sign your baby's name. Then sign your name and write your account number as you would with a check made out to you. Deposit the money in your own account and transfer it to your child's account later.

Ways to Save Money as a New Parent

The expenses of parenthood may take you by surprise. The sheer quantity of diapers alone may seem like a huge expense. There are ways to save money on your new expenses:

- Clip diaper, baby food, and formula coupons and ask friends and family to do so for you, too.
- Buy big at sales.

223
• • •

- Compare prices and shop at a warehouse club if you can get better prices there.
- Consider using store brands instead of name brands.

You can also sign up with the various diaper, formula, baby food, and baby product companies for coupons, special offers, and free samples. Most have e-newsletters that will include coupons. Try these websites:

- www.huggies.com
- www.pampers.com
- www.luvs.com
- www.enfamil.com
- www.brightbeginnings.com
- www.welcomeaddition.com
- www.naturesone.com
- www.gerber.com
- www.nestleusa.com
- www.playtexbaby.com
- www.beechnut.com
- www.earthsbest.com
- www.heinzbaby.com
- www.desitin.com
- www.johnsonsbaby.com
- www.balmex.com

Keep your eye out for special mail-in offers for formula and baby food. Manufacturers often have programs in which you can send in UPC symbols and get toys or rebates.

Even if you are breastfeeding, get the free formula samples that are available to you. In a few months you will start making cereal for your baby and can use formula in it instead of water or expressed breast milk. You can always donate unused formula to a food pantry or homeless shelter.

When you buy new products such as baby shampoo or diaper cream, buy the smallest quantities in case you don't care for it or your baby has a reaction to it. When you receive free samples of baby wipes, diaper cream, or diapers, put these in your diaper bag for on-the-go use.

Join Club Mom (www.clubmom.com) for free rewards as well as online chat rooms and tips for parents. If you register your credit cards and grocery discount cards with this site, you can earn rewards such as movie passes or free merchandise.

If your child goes to day care, you'll soon find that it is more expensive than you anticipated with all of the add-on expenses of things you are required to bring or provide. To save money on day care expenses:

- **Buy in bulk.** Buy diapers, wipes, formula, and baby food that you are responsible for bringing in bulk. Many centers require a certain number of items per week. Bring in a bulk pack and ask them to credit you for a month.
- **Buy vacation time.** Many centers give you one week of vacation per year. If you want more, you may be able to buy vacation time. Instead of paying the regular day rate, you can purchase extra vacation days in advance for a reduced price.
- **Ask about bartering.** If you or your partner provides a service or product the center might need, such as accounting, carpeting, landscaping, and so on, offer to barter these products or services in exchange for part of your costs.

If you use a nanny or sitter, you can save money by sharing a nanny with another family (for example, you could each use her for twenty hours a week and then each pay half of her wages). If you do not have a regular sitter or nanny, consider working out a babysitting agreement with a friend or neighbor. You watch her kids two days a week and she watches yours two days a week.

Updating Your Parenthood Budget

Now that you are a parent, you may find that your projected budget wasn't complete or accurate. Add in new expenses you find yourself incurring and compare expenses with income to make sure you can afford those expenses.

Your Lifestyle

Coming Home with Your Baby

Coming home from the hospital or birth center is one of those moments you will always remember. The days after you come home are filled with baby care and visitors. It can be wonderful to see all the people who are so happy to greet your new baby, but it can also be a lot of work. To make things easier on yourself:

- Don't worry about keeping the house in perfect condition. If you truly can't stand to let anyone see a less-than-perfect home, keep just the main living area clean.
- Ask people to stop at the grocery store and grab a few things on your list when they come by.
- Set a specific time period for a visit (i.e., from 1 P.M. to 2 P.M.) so that people know when to leave.
- Don't feel you have to feed everyone who comes. If you do want to provide food, have your partner pick up something premade at the store.
- Stash a comb, lip gloss, facial wipes, and any other beauty products you might want in a drawer in the living room or family room so you can pull yourself together for visitors without having to go upstairs or to the bathroom.
- Put a sign on the front door and turn off the phone if you don't want to be disturbed.
- Take people up on their offers to help. Let them throw in a load of laundry, do the dishes, or run the vacuum for you while they're there.
- If you need to nurse the baby and want privacy, leave the room or let them know it's time to go.

- Remind yourself that your focus is on your baby and not on cleaning or entertaining.

Shaken Baby Syndrome and Crying

You may have heard about Shaken Baby Syndrome in the news. Shaken Baby Syndrome is a medical condition caused by the violent shaking of a baby. Symptoms include vomiting or lethargy and more serious things such as coma or death. The National Center on Shaken Baby Syndrome (www.dontshake.com) reports that it can take only twenty seconds of shaking to cause damage. Most parents would never do anything to harm their baby, but it's important to understand the seriousness of this syndrome and the frustration that often leads to it. There has been some speculation that it could be caused by rough play, such as bouncing a child up and down on your knee or throwing him or her in the air. Shaken Baby Syndrome is most common from six weeks to four months of age —when crying is most frequent.

Crying is the most common reason parents or caregivers shake a baby. According to the National Institutes of Health, babies under four months cry two to three hours a day, with 20 percent

Books About Babies and Crying

The Happiest Baby on the Block: The New Way to Calm Crying and Help Your Newborn Baby Sleep Longer by Harvey Karp (Bantam, 2003, $13.95).

The No-Cry Sleep Solution by Elizabeth Pantley (McGraw-Hill, 2002, $12.95).

Secrets of the Baby Whisperer: How to Calm, Connect, and Communicate with Your Baby by Melinda Blau (Ballantine, 2002, $13.95).

to 30 percent of babies crying even longer. You're going to have to deal with the crying and understand that when it happens, you will feel stressed out, exhausted, overwhelmed, and frustrated. But if you know this going in, you can plan out the steps to take to help you deal with the crying. And you can remember that this period of development won't last forever.

Dealing with Postpartum Depression

Postpartum depression (PPD) is a serious illness, but it is something that can be treated successfully. It's important to recognize the signs and symptoms so that you can seek treatment if it happens to you. According to The National Women's Health Information Center (NWHIC) at the U.S. Department of Health and Human Services, the signs of postpartum depression include:

- Restlessness or irritability
- A feeling of sadness, depression, or uncontrollable crying
- A lack of or loss of energy
- Headaches, chest pains, heart palpitations (the heart beating fast and feeling like it is skipping beats), numbness, or hyperventilation (fast and shallow breathing)
- Sleeplessness or lethargy, or both
- A loss of appetite and rapid weight loss
- Overeating and weight gain
- Memory problems or inability to focus and make decisions
- Excessive worrying about the baby
- A lack of interest in the baby
- A feeling of worthlessness and guilt
- Being afraid of hurting the baby or yourself
- A decrease in interest or pleasure in activities, including sex

A woman may feel anxious after childbirth but not have PPD. She may have what is called *postpartum anxiety* or *panic disorder*. According to NWHIC, the signs of this condition include a strong anxiety and/or fear, rapid breathing, a fast heart rate, hot or cold flashes, chest pain, and feeling shaky or dizzy. Talk with your health care provider right away if you have any of these signs. Medication and counseling can be used to treat postpartum anxiety. For help or information, contact Depression After Delivery at 800-944-4773, or at: www.DepressionAfterDelivery.com.

Changing Your Work Schedule/Your Partner's Work Schedule as Your Life Changes

You may find that as your child grows, you want to change your work schedule to optimize your time with him or her. Within a year your baby's needs and schedule will be very different, so don't assume that the current schedule will be set in stone. Remember that you can take an FMLA leave every year to provide care for a child who is ill.

Taking a Baby to Work

Most employers do not permit employees to bring their children to work with them. You might be able to arrange for your baby to be brought to you for feeding once or twice during the day without causing any great disruption, but in general, it's too difficult to have your child with you at work. The exception is if you work at a day care where you may be able to bring your child for a reduced fee while you are working.

On-Site Day Care

If your employer offers on-site day care, get on the waiting list as soon as you know you are pregnant or know you will return to work. On-site day care allows you to be close to your baby so that you can check in on him or her several times during the day and breastfeed if you wish. When your child is older, you may be able to have lunch with him or her. On-site day care is also often less

229
• • •

expensive than off-site care, since the employer often subsidizes a portion of the cost.

A fifteen-page list of employer-supported day care centers is available for a fee online at: www.workfamily.com/open/spec_desc .asp.

Working Mother magazine also creates a yearly list of the 100 best employers for working mothers. Find it on their website at: www.workingmother.com, in the "Working Mother Exclusives" section.

Coping with Stress

Working and parenting can be overwhelming. It's important to remember that it is going to take you some time to adjust to working and caring for a child. Some parents have a difficult time emotionally. If you trust the person caring for your baby, you can reassure yourself that he or she is safe. Checking in once a day by phone or in person can help you feel connected and involved. When you pick up your child, get details about what he or she did during the day and find out how much he or she ate and slept. Leaving your child in someone else's care can be very difficult, but you can and will adjust to it.

Getting Enough Sleep

It can be hard to get enough sleep when you're the parent of a baby. There are several things you can do to help you maximize your sleep time and deal with a lack of sleep.

The National Sleep Foundation recommends:

- Getting enough exercise
- Finishing eating two to three hours before trying to sleep
- Avoiding nicotine, alcohol, and caffeine close to bedtime
- Taking short breaks at work if you are tired when you are there

Michael J. Breus, Ph.D., diplomate of The American Board of Sleep Medicine and cofounder of SoundSleepSolutions.com suggests trying the following:

• Take catnaps (no longer than thirty to forty-five minutes) during your lunch break when at work or while at home with the baby if you're exhausted. Naps longer than this will be deep sleep and it is much harder to wake up.

• Cut out watching TV or using a computer at night and instead focus on getting more sleep. Even the light from a laptop can influence the circadian rhythm of an individual's sleeping patterns.

• Try to get things done when the baby is awake so you can sleep when he or she is asleep. Give yourself a window of thirty minutes or so after the baby is asleep to get things done, then use the rest of the time to sleep.

• Simplify your life and do only those things that have to be done. If you have a choice between vacuuming and sleeping, for example, pick sleeping. If it makes you too anxious to skip doing something, though, you will sleep better if you just get it done. So, for example, if you are a clean freak you might not be able to let the vacuuming go, but you could skip calling your mom back that night.

• Try to catch up on sleep on the weekends or at a time when the other parent can watch your baby.

• Get a friend or relative to babysit for a few hours once a week so you can sleep.

• Be careful driving when you are very tired. If you ever feel as though you might fall asleep at the wheel, pull over immediately. Most new parents are sleep deprived and this can have a huge effect on your reaction time. If you feel tired when you get in the car, be late for work or cancel your appointment so you can get some sleep.

• Pull the window shades or wear a sleep mask to help you nap during daylight hours. Soft music or earplugs (with a decibel rated at or below 32db, so you can still hear the baby crying) can also help.

Coping with Stay-at-Home Parenting

If you have chosen to stay home and care for your baby, you probably have found that it is something you are still adjusting to. Caring for your child is a very busy job, but it is one that can sometimes leave you feeling a little disconnected from the rest of the world.

To enjoy and make the most of this new and fulfilling job, the National Association of At-Home Mothers recommends:

- Develop new friends who are doing the same thing you are. Visit local playgrounds, attend Mommy and Me classes, or chat online.
- If you're really feeling the decrease in income because you left your job, think about ways you can earn money from home.
- Give yourself tasks to accomplish each week. When you successfully accomplish them, you will feel as though you have achieved something.
- Reduce your expectations. It's impossible to have a spotless home, cook gourmet meals, and raise a happy and healthy child. Prioritize and don't feel guilty for the things you let slip.
- Do something each day for yourself, whether it is reading a magazine, taking a bath, or having coffee with a friend.
- Don't compare yourself to other women or to your partner. Remember that the job you are doing is important and you're doing the best you can do.

Single Parenting

If you're parenting your baby alone, develop a support system. You can't and shouldn't try to do everything yourself. Let friends and family babysit or come over to help you so you can get a break. The key to making single parenting manageable is having realistic expectations for yourself. Keep these tips in mind:

- Plan time for yourself in your schedule. You are a person first and a parent second.
- See yourself as part of a large extended family made up of family and friends who can help you. Don't be afraid to rely on them.
- Expect some things to be difficult on your own but know that you will manage and you will get through it.
- Do things to make your life easier, such as ordering groceries and diapers online, getting takeout, and letting the housekeeping go once in a while.
- Have someone available that you can call in the middle of the night when the baby has been screaming for hours and you think you're about ready to lose it.
- Arm yourself with some good parenting books when you need to turn to an expert.

For single parenting support, contact Parents Without Partners at: www.parentswithoutpartners.com, or use my book *How to Parent with Your Ex: Working Together for Your Child's Best Interest* (Sourcebooks, 2005) for support and information.

Learning How to Pack

If you're like most new parents, you want to be prepared at all times. But this can lead to overpacking and a diaper bag that weighs more than your child. Whether you're heading out for a few hours, a day, a weekend, or a week, be realistic about what you need to take. If you're going to the mall, you probably don't need more than a small diaper bag with a few diapers, a small changing pad, some wipes, and some toys for older babies. Some parents find it is helpful to buy a small diaper bag to use for quick trips to the store and save the big diaper bag for longer outings. If you can't help but plan for the "what-ifs," pack an emergency diaper bag to keep in your car. Here are some things you could fill it with:

233

- A change of clothes for the baby
- A clean top for yourself
- Extra diapers
- Extra wipes
- Diaper cream
- Jars of unopened baby food and a spoon
- Toys
- A blanket
- A bottle of water
- An unopened can of formula and a bottle
- An unopened container of juice

If you have more than one child, a backpack diaper bag might make more sense for you. Diaper bags tend to slide off shoulders, and if you're trying to hold a toddler's or preschooler's hand and manage a baby, a diaper bag that stays put is invaluable. It can also be helpful to condense the contents of your purse and diaper bag into one bag.

Develop a routine that you will always follow when you leave the house so that you don't forget anything. For example, always grab the pacifier before you get your keys. Or make sure that every time you come home you restock your diaper bag so that it will be ready to go the next time.

Planning a Christening, Bris, or Other Celebration

If you plan to have a religious ceremony to welcome your baby, talk to your clergy member about scheduling it. If you will be having a party after the ceremony, or if you are planning a "meet the new addition" party, remember that you are still recovering from the birth and should not overdo things. Try the following:

- Buy most of the food for the party instead of cooking.
- Use paper and plastic plates and utensils.
- Have the party outside, if at all possible.
- Communicate to all guests the hours the party will last.

- Wear something comfortable that makes you feel fabulous.
- Ask close relatives and friends to help out by bringing food and paper goods and to help with setting up and cleaning up.

Baby Announcements, Gifts, and Thank-Yous

The simplest way to spread the news about your baby is to put a message on your answering machine so that anyone who calls can get the basic information. You might also want to send out an e-mail announcement soon after the baby is born.

Free e-mail announcements are available online at:

- www.happygreetings.net
- www.babyzone.com/features/cards/card.asp

To get a free official White House greeting for your baby, send his or her name, address, and date of birth to:

White House Greetings Office
Room 39
Washington, DC 20500

Web-savvy parents might want to create a Web page with photos and birth information so everyone can get a peek at the new baby. You can set up free birth announcement Web pages online at:

- www.babababies.com
- www.babiesonline.com
- www.growthspurts.com

If you choose a printed announcement, be aware that it will take a few weeks for the order to be filled. Some parents create their own announcements on the computer and mail them out themselves.

You can find templates for printed birth announcements online at:

- http://desktoppub.about.com/library/templates/blwrapper
  baby.htm
- www.happygreetings.net/birthann/printableBirthAnnounce
  mentsCards.php

If you would like to create special handmade announcements, you can find templates at: www.marthastewart.com/page.jhtml? type=content&id=channel1265.

Baby gifts will start to roll in, and despite how busy you are, you should keep a running list so you can remember who sent each item and send thank-yous later. Give yourself permission to get rid of gifts you will never use. Use the chart below to record gifts you receive from friends, family members, or visitors or at religious ceremonies.

BABY GIFT LOG

Name of Gift Giver	Item	Date Thank-You Sent

Name of Gift Giver	Item	Date Thank-You Sent
_____	_____	_____
_____	_____	_____
_____	_____	_____
_____	_____	_____
_____	_____	_____
_____	_____	_____
_____	_____	_____
_____	_____	_____
_____	_____	_____
_____	_____	_____
_____	_____	_____
_____	_____	_____
_____	_____	_____
_____	_____	_____
_____	_____	_____
_____	_____	_____
_____	_____	_____

Try to write thank-you notes as soon as possible after you receive the gift. The longer you wait, the harder they are to write. If you made up address labels on the computer for your shower, print them out again and use them to send the thank-you notes. Some ideas for thank-you notes include:

- Taking a photo of the baby with the gift and writing a short note on the back and mailing it off
- Photocopying the baby's footprint onto colored paper and writing a thank-you underneath it
- Taking a digital photo of the baby and including a copy with each thank-you note
- Taking a photo of the baby with the gift giver and sending a copy with the thank-you note

Ideas to Make Life Easier

Life with a new baby can be complicated. Try some of these tips to make things easier:

- Set up diaper changing areas on both floors if you have a two-story home.
- Do laundry more often. Try throwing a load in each time you run the dishwasher—this way you won't forget. It's easier to find the time to do one load than it is to find the time to do five loads all at once.
- Choose one day a week to deal with bills, money, and bank accounts. It can be easy to forget about due dates and payments in the first few weeks of parenthood, but if you set aside every Friday night to spend some time on it, it won't be forgotten. You can also write the due dates for bills on your calendar or keep them in a folder, organized in order of when their payments are due. Write the due date on the return envelope and put the payment stub inside so all you need to do is write the check or pay it online.
- Always keep extra supplies of diapers, laundry detergent, dishwashing detergent, toilet paper, and other items on hand. When you use one up, buy a new backup so that you won't run out.

- Get enough sleep. Take naps during the day and don't feel like you should use times when the baby is sleeping to always do something productive. Sleeping more will make you more productive.
- Use paper plates and cups for a few weeks or during a really colicky period. The extra dollars you'll spend will be well worth the convenience.
- Use your answering machine. Turn off the ringer on the phone if you need to sleep and let the machine take calls when you are resting, feeding the baby, or just relaxing.
- Simplify your life. Don't plan on planting a full vegetable garden, decorating your house from top to bottom for the holidays, buying personalized gifts for graduations or birthdays, or making all your meals from scratch while you have a young baby. This is the time in your life to cut corners, take shortcuts, and not worry about what anyone will think.

Dealing with Advice

People love to give advice to new parents. There are plenty of people who will think they know your baby better than you do. It's hard to have confidence when you're doing something that is so new to you and so different from anything else you've ever experienced, but you'll find that you do know what you're doing, and what you don't know, you will figure out. If you're looking for advice, you can get some good tips from other moms or from your parents. Not everything will work with every baby, though.

If you're getting unsolicited advice, there are several ways to handle it. If you're receiving unsolicited advice from strangers, often the best course is to smile and agree and then go on to care for your baby as you wish. When you're getting ongoing advice from relatives, sometimes you can just shrug it off, but other times you have to be aggressive and say thanks but no thanks.

239
...

Parenthood Checklist
- [ ] Update your will.
- [ ] Change your life insurance beneficiary.
- [ ] Familiarize yourself with required immunizations.

- [ ] Complete a medical authorization form.
- [ ] Complete form authorizing others to pick up your child from day care.
- [ ] Find out your employer's policy about breastfeeding and pumping at work.
- [ ] Plan out a pumping schedule if you will be returning to work.
- [ ] Read your state's breastfeeding laws.
- [ ] Apply for a social security number for your baby.
- [ ] Adjust your payroll withholding for dependents.
- [ ] Open a bank account for your baby.
- [ ] Develop a long-term financial plan for your baby.
- [ ] Open a college savings account.
- [ ] Sign up for discounts, coupons, and special offers for parents.
- [ ] Update your parenthood budget.
- [ ] Pack an emergency bag for the car.
- [ ] Plan your bris, christening, or other celebration.
- [ ] Send birth announcements.
- [ ] Keep track of gifts you receive.
- [ ] Send thank-you notes.

Index